More God

From The Twelve Steps Into Deeper Faith

Constance Bovier

Xulon PRESS

Xulon Press
11350 Random Hills Road
Suite 800
Fairfax, VA 22030
(703) 279-6511
XulonPress.com

Contents

Acknowledgements

I owe my enduring thanks to two Twelve Step friends, Gisela and Sherry, whose timely "How's the book coming?" often kept me on task, even when I didn't want to be. I'm also grateful to the women of my Tuesday morning breakfast group, committed Christians all, who listened, encouraged and loved me throughout the writing and publishing processes.

Finally, I thank my husband Pete Wolfe, a remarkable man who believed in me from the start. I will always stand in awe of his remarkable gift for nurturing dreams and inspiring achievement in those around him. Including me.

Foreword

by John Thomason, Pastor
St. John's United Methodist Church
Texas City, Texas

═══════════════════════════

Having grown up in the church, my first experiences of God happened to be in a conventional religious setting. Those experiences eventually led me in the direction of ordained ministry. I've served as a pastor for 25 years, and still believe that Christian faith and church participation are viable ways to have communion with God. At the same time, I understand that many of my fellow humans start in other places and follow other paths.

I learned about Twelve Step spirituality as a young parish pastor when I began to have contact with individuals in recovery from various addictions. I listened to their moving accounts of struggle, breakthrough and perseverance, sometimes even heard their Fifth Steps as part of the healing process. Of course, I was the "pastoral counselor," the "helping professional" in the relationship. Yet I received far more than I gave in these exchanges.

Hearing individuals describe their struggles with addiction, I was astounded by the similarity of their stories with my own efforts to control or change certain aspects of my behavior. I had to admit that I, too, had experienced powerlessness and unmanageability. I, too, had sought to medicate feelings and escape reality. I, too, had suffered the consequences of my own harmful behaviors—and still been unable to stop them. Far from feeling superior to recovering addicts, I felt a mysterious kinship with them.

Strangely enough, I identified more with the problem than with the solution they described. There I was, an ordained minister, fluent in the language of religion, yet the spiritual experiences reported by recovering people sounded as foreign to me as an obscure dialect. I came to realize these individuals had plumbed a depth of spirituality I knew little about. I became intrigued by the "steps" they were taking to turn their lives over to God and, in so doing, actually overcome their addictions.

In short order, the Twelve Steps became a vital part of my life, not just as a technique for helping others, but as a pattern for my own self-care and spiritual growth. Over the years I've served as a chaplain in a chemical dependency treatment facility and counseled many other addicts in the local church setting. But my primary tie to Twelve Step spirituality is personal, not professional. I practice the steps because I need them to keep my own house in order, and because they have opened the door to a relationship with God that I never thought would be possible.

I first got acquainted with Connie Bovier in the context of a traditional community of faith. I soon discovered that her spirituality both incorporates and transcends the traditional. She and I spoke comfortably to each other in the language of religion, but we also discovered that we share the common "dialect" of recovery and the spiritual quest that goes with it. When Connie's quest was written in book form, she asked me to read the manuscript and write the foreword. I was enormously honored to do so.

A spiritual mentor of mine once observed that religion has a remarkably simple starting point. It begins with the perception of "something more"—of a reality beyond time and space, and yet part of our everyday experience; something that gives order, direction and purpose to all creation and especially to human life.

The book you are about to read is the story of Connie Bovier's search for that "something more." She initially found God, not in the incense-filled pews of the church, but in the smoke-filled rooms of Twelve Step groups. Had her spiritual journey ended there, it would have been worthwhile, but not nearly as fascinating and enriching as it became when she pushed on. After developing authentic spirituality, Connie found that she wanted even more, and her search led her back to her spiritual roots in Christian faith and the church. Finding both spirituality *and* religion, she creatively integrated the two.

In the Eleventh Step of Alcoholics Anonymous, recovering persons pledge "through prayer and meditation to improve [their] conscious contact with God." Traditional religion became an unexpected ally in Connie's effort to reach this goal. She not only understands what William James called "the varieties of religious experience," she has experienced many of these varieties herself. Rather than flitting compulsively from one spiritual fad to another without ever making a commitment, she instead conveys a genuine passion to know God and a willingness to meet God on God's turf, which may be anywhere!

In recent years Connie's desire to know God more intimately has led her to places and experiences that go far beyond the spiritual exploration of most church members. Where she goes and how she gets there are two of the delightful surprises that await you in this book.

If you're looking for "something more" than standard fare in your spiritual or religious reading, I trust you'll find Connie's story to be suggestive and hopeful. Likewise, helping professionals of all types will recognize how the Twelve Steps enhance the recovery potential of their clients. Therapists will see the value of spiritual resources in the healing process. Clergy will be gratified to know that Twelve Step spirituality and traditional faith are parallel in purpose and can work together to transform troubled lives.

I believe this book will illumine the path of all who seek "more God" on their spiritual journeys.

Introduction

Since 1981 I've attended an estimated 5,000 meetings of Twelve Step recovery groups. That's about 5,000 hours spent in rooms with other people, talking about God.

Newcomers to Twelve Step fellowships are often put off by the emphasis on God in the meetings and in the steps. Some are none too pleased to hear that millions have found reliance on a Higher Power their only effective solution for dependence on alcohol, drugs, gambling, food, tobacco or a host of other compulsive/addictive problems.

Some people explore this unfamiliar territory grudgingly. Many find amazing relief from addiction and, if they're diligent in working the Twelve Steps, a measure of improvement in other areas of their lives as well.

Some people consider that enough.

I call it settling for the first miracle.

The men and women I've admired most in recovery are those who go much further. They're people who mine the Twelve Steps for every bit of spiritual guidance they can dig out, and then reach beyond for more spiritual growth.

There was Evelyn, a woman of remarkable grace and

courage. When I listened to Evelyn in meetings, I marveled at her reliance on God and how it produced in her the resilience to live with a still-drinking alcoholic husband. There was Sarah, physically disabled from birth, who expressed so much love and unshakable faith that she calmed the atmosphere of every meeting she attended. And there was Jim, dying of leukemia, who went right on sharing his experience and expressing his gratitude to God until the end.

These and others like them are my heroes—the men and women who refuse to settle for God's first miracle when so much more awaits.

The story that follows traces my own faith journey.

I don't speak for any Twelve Step program. I write solely from personal experience. As much as I'd like to credit the three fellowships that have changed my life, I choose not to name them, respecting the principle of anonymity which discourages members from specific identification with Twelve Step programs in public forums. I especially want to ensure that nothing I say may tarnish or embarrass any of the fellowships that have changed my life.

I have written this book first of all out of gratitude to God. And for God. After all it is his story, lived out through me.

Second, I've written this book for the imaginary readers who've stood by patiently as my words ticked out across the computer screen.

Perhaps *More God* may provide some insight into the spiritual foundation that can be built in the often profane, always love-filled rooms of Twelve Step recovery. It is my hope that these pages will offer encouragement to others to explore for themselves the unlimited potential for spiritual growth that lies just one step beyond Twelve Step doors.

Connie Bovier
Houston, Texas, 2002

Spiritual Snapshots

"When we speak of spiritual matters, especially
when we mention God, we have re-opened a subject which
(the newcomer) thought he had neatly evaded or entirely
ignored....We know how he feels....we imagined
we had abandoned the God idea entirely."
Alcoholics Anonymous (The Big Book)

1950. Tibbetts Methodist Church in West Seattle. I'm sitting in the pew beside my older sister and my grandmother, fidgeting against the prickly seams of my slip and dress. (Few garments escape my determined mother's starch bottle.) The church is cold. I am miserable. Obligatory church attendance is the only bad part about spending a weekend with my paternal grandparents.

1954. A tiny church in Eugene, Oregon. Denomination unknown. I sit in a Sunday school class, struggling to comprehend what's going on. The teacher uses words I don't understand. She passes out something that looks like play money with *talent* printed on it. I must have missed the lesson that explained about *talents*. I'm relieved when the hour ends. I meet my sister outside where we watch for Dad's arrival to pick us up. I carry my *talent* home, wondering what I'm supposed to do with it.

1968. Wando Woods Baptist Church, Charleston, South Carolina. I wheel into the parking lot just in time to scoop my son and daughter from the stream of kids tumbling out of Sunday school. I hustle Troy and Kelly into the car. We make our escape. *Whew.* One more parental duty accomplished. Now that's done, I can get on with the rest of the day.

1970. An apartment north of Washington, D.C. My husband (the first of three) is talking about religion. I squirm at his beliefs. He's headed for hell, he tells me, because it's too late to make up for years of backsliding. (That's what *he* learned as a child.) Unsettled by his views, unable to marshal clear beliefs of my own, I resolve to avoid future discussions about God. Evasion seems the reasonable way to deal with such a disquieting topic.

1981. Webb's Chapel United Methodist Church in Farmers Branch, a northwest suburb of Dallas. I walk into the room where my Twelve Step group meets only to find a dozen strangers arranging centerpieces and setting tables for a church event. They cheerfully direct me to the temporary location for my meeting.

The chapel.

The *chapel*?

I agonize for long minutes in the hall.

My desperation has driven me to a church because that's where the Twelve Step program I need holds its meetings.

But sitting in a fellowship hall is a far cry from meeting in a *chapel*.

My stomach clenches in a resistant knot.

To heck with the meeting, I *almost* tell myself.

I *almost* turn to leave.

* * *

I am hardly unique in taking an extended detour away from religion. I know countless others who've ventured far afield for many years.

Sometimes I've been mystified by the bumpy road I have followed back to faith.

My return to God, or more accurately *my initiation into a practical, working belief in God*, has been less a series of neat, chronological events than a circuitous route through loosely linked thematic experiences.

As a child I was nominally acquainted with spiritual matters. My parents taught me to say my prayers ... *now I lay me down to sleep*. My big sister Carol and I had a guardian angel to watch over us. (I was so terrified by that glow-in-the-dark angel that I covered my head to fall asleep ... but that's another story.)

Was it the starch in my clothes or in my diminutive grandmother's spine that made me so uncomfortable sitting in church? Was I alienated by the confusing variety of Sunday schools I attended as my family moved about Washington and Oregon while I was growing up? Or was my avoidance of God grounded in the guilt I felt for sending my own children to Sunday school rather than attending church with them?

It seemed that I never got the point about religion. I don't recall anything about it ever feeling particularly good.

I was well into my forties when I confessed to my mother how spooked I'd been by the luminous angel on my bedroom wall when I was five. We laughed, but I could see that she would have liked to go back and make it better. "Why didn't you tell me?" she asked. "Why didn't you say something about it?"

Well, I *was* saying something about it. Granted, a bit late. But I honestly couldn't tell Mother why I'd never mentioned my fear all those years ago.

I've decided it doesn't matter.

I've also decided that it's not important to cobble together a rational explanation for my years of spiritual wandering. Analyzing reasons may be an interesting intellectual exercise but it seldom generates useful results.

There is one pertinent question, however, a question that lies at the heart of my life: *How in heaven's name did I get from where I once was to where I am today?*

How in heaven's name indeed!

Photography Lesson

Had someone described to me years ago the person I was to become, I would have laughed in disbelief. Yet the pictures etched in my mind have captured as clearly as any photo album my internal surrender, the gradual opening of my mind and the spiritual transformation that have taken place over my twenty years in Twelve Step recovery.

Soggy Surrender

"In everyone's psyche there exists an unconquerable ego
which bitterly opposes any thought of defeat."
Alcoholics Anonymous Comes of Age

Susan was crying again.

My friend Gisela grumbled under her breath as we found
two empty chairs at the table. We were a few minutes late
and our favorite Tuesday noon meeting was already underway. Susan was sharing and, as usual, a pile of soggy tissues
was mounding up on the table in front of her. Gisela, a no-
nonsense German, had little sympathy for emotional excess.

Sheepishly Susan apologized for her tears. She said she
didn't understand why she couldn't stop crying. She said
she'd been in Twelve Step recovery for several months and
still cried every time she talked in a meeting. You'd think
she'd get over it, she said.

Gisela muttered in agreement as she rummaged in her
purse for a dollar to toss into the basket circulating around
the table.

Ignoring my grumpy friend, I watched Susan. Something important was happening. Though her waterworks seemed to lack a shutoff valve, I saw that she was at a critical juncture in recovery. I recognized her tears because I'd been there myself. I'd never cried so often or for so long and rarely in meetings, but I'd certainly used my share of tissues during my tenure in the Twelve Steps. In the process I'd learned the value of tears.

* * *

A fan of science fiction since high school, I once read an entertaining novel about an alien race invading and dominating the earth. Although the aliens were benevolent their takeover exacted a terrible toll on humanity. The only concession the overlords demanded was an outward recognition of their supremacy. But humans, being human, continued to resist. Mankind couldn't, simply *wouldn't,* admit defeat.

The word *surrender* rings positively un-American to those of us immersed in our culture of can-do individualism. I know it sounded that way to me.

I was raised in a family where a favorite adage was, "Never say can't" and years later I repeated the same words to my own children. Yet by age forty, when I found myself incapable of reining in my addictive behaviors, our stoic family motto did me little good.

Believe me, if I could have stopped my self-destructive compulsions with my own determination I would have done so. I had no interest in devoting countless hours and who knew how much energy to some self-help program, not when I thought that everything in my life was going just fine except for a couple of little problems.

But it was only when I picked up the telephone and called one of the "anonymous" programs listed in the phone book, only when I wrote down the time and location of the nearest meeting, only when I made up my mind to attend that meeting no matter what ... only then did I begin to experience relief.

My first surrender.

Few people walk into their first Twelve Step meetings happy to be there. Distress is the common denominator. Some people are rebellious. Some are embarrassed. Some are in despair. I was confused and afraid.

The lucky ones among us are at our wits end. We already know we can't solve our problem alone. And we don't know where else to turn for help.

Surely recovering addicts of every kind are among the most blessed people on earth, not because of any earned grace, but because we're forced by our circumstances to seek God, and because God hears and responds to every sincere admission of defeat. At the moment of surrender God has room to step in with the first miracle—the power to abstain from addiction.

* * *

Surrender is a tough enough concept for people in Twelve Step programs to grasp. It can be nearly impossible for those outside the program to comprehend. I've seen the skeptical looks and furrowed brows of my family and friends when I've attempted to describe the Twelve Step surrender process. My own mother missed the point. After I was in recovery for a number of years, she told me about a mutual friend who shared one of my addictions. "She'd be all right," Mother said, "if only she'd muster up some willpower."

The solution for addicts, however, never lies in developing *more* willpower. In fact, the Twelve Step solution is centered on *giving up* one's own will in favor of God's will. That's the foundation for recovery.

It's perfectly okay, of course, that my mother and most

other people don't get the necessity for surrender as the Twelve Step programs practice it. They don't need to get it. They're not locked in grim combat against life-threatening, spirit-killing addictions.

Nonetheless, surrender is a powerful tool for dealing with a host of other life problems—difficulties that are hardly the exclusive domain of Twelve Steppers.

Surrender is the means by which I open my soul to the ministrations of the great healer.

Surrender is the only way I've discovered to deal with emotional pain.

And tears by the bucketful are often part of it.

* * *

On a bleak Saturday afternoon in January, 1990, my grown children and some friends helped my soon-to-be-ex-second-husband and me move furniture and boxes to the North Dallas apartment that I would call my new home.

This husband and I had spent ten years trying to make our marriage work. Even though I had nine years of Twelve Step recovery and I'd been trying to apply all the principles for healthy relationships that I'd been learning, we'd been mismatched from the start. I was willing to seek counseling (anything!) but he had decided it was time we put the struggle behind us.

We were being adult about it, of course. He would keep the house, along with our Great Dane and our black Manx cat who thought he owned the neighborhood. I would take the Siamese and calico cats whom we felt would adapt well to apartment life.

The tough part came after we'd delivered the last load of bookcases and books and dismissed our helpers. I drove back to the house one final time for last minute items and the cats.

When Jellybean and Miss Astor were corralled and

secured in their carriers, I turned to my husband. Aching for the imagined comfort of a final embrace, I held out my arms.

Misery clouded his face. He shook his head. In a voice I barely recognized, he said, "Just go, Connie. *Go.*"

I don't remember the three mile drive from the house where I'd lived for years to my new apartment. I don't remember parking my car, going inside or releasing the cats from their carriers to explore our new home. I do remember sinking to my knees amidst the sea of cartons and leaning against one of the boxes to cry.

This was no gentle weeping, but huge, wracking sobs, emerging from pain that felt unbearable. How long did I cry, kneeling there in a strange apartment where I didn't want to be? Five minutes? Fifteen?

Even grieving the loss of a husband I still loved, even dampening a carton with tears, I knew I wouldn't plummet into a bottomless chasm of despair. The relationship I'd been developing with God for nine years had convinced me otherwise.

Still, I was at a major turning point. Would I choose the seemingly easy route around the pain by seeking immediate solace in other people, in distracting activities, in relapse into addiction? Or would I choose to deepen my dependence upon God by staying with the pain until I felt his strength?

I prayed.

Like a wave subsides, so did the sorrow. I knew there would be more tears to shed and I would handle those when they came. But for that moment I was cleansed.

Alone. Empty. Exhausted.

And ready for God's healing touch.

Standing up, I wiped my face, blew my nose and took a deep breath.

Then I set up my coffeepot and arranged food and water for the cats in my tiny new kitchen. Opening a carton of linens, I carried my pillow and sheets into the bedroom to make my bed and begin my new life.

* * *

One of the last times Gisela and I attended our favorite Tuesday meeting together, we saw Susan again. When it was her turn to share, one of the group regulars delighted everyone by reaching under the table and, with a mischievous grin, handing Susan a thick bath towel for her tears.

Everyone laughed.

Susan laughed.

Even Gisela, who'd been softening up lately, laughed.

Not long afterward, Gisela suffered a massive heart attack and brain stem stroke. She wasn't expected to live. Her husband and I huddled over her bed in intensive care. In the waiting room we talked about finalities in shock-dulled voices.

By a miracle, Gisela survived. She eventually transferred to a rehabilitation hospital, but it was many weeks before she emerged from her coma, more weeks before she was able to sit in a wheelchair and to speak.

One evening as a nurse pushed her wheelchair into the hospital dining room, she offered to wheel Gisela across the room to sit with several other people. Eyes crossed, barely upright, scarcely able to talk, Gisela glared at the other wheelchair patients across the room and blurted, "I don't want to sit with those people. They're defective!"

So she ate her meals alone.

Eventually the crying began. Everyone assured Gisela that tears were a common side effect of strokes. There was nothing unusual in what was happening to her. But it was hard for an emotionally tough German to find herself out of control. For a while, it seemed, she wept over everything. And many of her tears were shed in response to the dawning knowledge that she too was defective, and likely to remain so.

Today Gisela tells this story on herself. She uses it to illustrate the dramatic change that's taken place in her life. She's been reborn—spiritually as well as physically, shedding thick layers of pride and arrogance as she's come to terms with the disabilities that are now an ongoing part of her life. Another surrender. At a deeper level. At a frightening cost.

Today Gisela navigates about with a walker or a quad cane. She often drives herself to the doctor, to local errands and to and from her Twelve Step meetings. Her indomitable attitude and unquenchable belief in God are inspiration to everyone around her.

And to me. I've learned much at the side of this woman, my best friend.

How many tears are enough?

As many as it takes.

Surrender Lesson

Tears are the precious lubricant of recovery for they signify a readiness to change. When tears spring from the deep well of surrender they can wash away every obstacle that chokes up the channel leading to God. Only when I am defeated physically, emotionally or spiritually—only then does God have the opening he wants for reaching all the way to my soul, where true change and lasting healing can begin.

Dreading Dad

"I have lately realized that what went wrong for me in my
Christian upbringing is centered in the belief that one had
to be dressed up, both outwardly and inwardly, to meet
God, the insidious notion that I need be a firm and
even cheerful believer before I dare show
my face in 'His' church."
Kathleen Norris
The Cloister Walk

My father was coming to visit and I was plenty worried.

For almost a decade I had lived on the east coast where
three thousand miles, modest incomes and prohibitive travel
costs had kept our visits to a minimum. Then in 1975, con-
current with my first divorce, I'd relocated to Dallas to be
near my two sisters and their families. Now Dad was making a trip from our original family home in the Pacific
Northwest to see us all.

I wasn't sure what to expect from his visit, but every day
the knot in my stomach tightened. In the years since I'd

grown up and moved away after high school my father had changed. He'd become religious. *Very* religious. I'd squirmed through countless letters and phone calls as he enthused about his church and his faith. Chaffing at the change I'd often wished for the familiar Dad, the highly principled, but decidedly secular man, who'd raised my sisters and me.

Worst of all, this new father ended all communications with a reminder that he was praying for me.

So there I was in Dallas, newly divorced, a thirty-some-thing, single mom of a twelve-year-old daughter and thirteen-year-old son. I was working at an exciting job as an advertising agency writer, leading an exhilarating nightlife on the dance floors of country and western honky-tonks and spending Sunday mornings sleeping in.

As the date of Dad's visit neared, I tried to convince myself that my sisters would serve as buffers. Our plan was to divide Dad's vacation time between their two homes, with evening and weekend visits to my apartment. Since Carol and Marlyn and their families all attended church, I figured Dad could talk to *them* about religion. That should get all the holy talk out of his system before he came to see me.

Still, I had some nagging doubts. There was always the chance that my sisters' churchiness would spur Dad to work on me (the last religious holdout) harder than before.

Concerns aside, I'd always loved my father and that was my overriding emotion the day I opened my door to welcome him.

We got off to a great start. After all, we had years of catching up to do. Dad got reacquainted with Troy and Kelly who hadn't seen their grandfather since they were pre-schoolers. Eventually the kids wandered off to their own activities, leaving Dad and me alone at the kitchen table. Draining a pot of coffee we exhausted one topic after another. We discussed my new career and then my divorce. Dad's compassionate concern for my ex-husband, as well as for the kids and me, reminded me of the unconditional love he'd shown at other difficult points in my life.

He must have sensed a good opening and soon he was off and running about God.

He talked about his church and the people who attended there, about the preacher, the music director, the evangelists who visited. It seemed as if he talked for hours.

My defenses rose like the mercury in a thermometer. I nodded and murmured vague comments and struggled to find a balance between rejection and encouragement. Whenever I sensed the end of a story, I shifted the conversation elsewhere. It worked several times. But never for long.

My father was like a compass, always pointing true north. Over and over, he returned to his faith and what his relationship with God meant in his life.

By the time Dad got around to the miraculous healings he and my stepmother had experienced, I was poised in my chair like a coiled spring. Every hair on my body stood on end. I longed to jump from my skin and bolt from the room.

But love and respect for my father won out. I stayed in my chair. Finally his evangelistic engine ran out of steam and stopped on its own.

The visit from my father that summer underscored three important points. One: We shared the same love we'd had for one another when I was a child. Two: The only thing that kept him from being *wonderful* was all this religious stuff. And three: church apparently served a purpose for people who didn't have the resources to deal with life alone. But I didn't want or need any part of it.

* * *

Somewhere in the gap between my childhood attendance at Sunday school and my adult entry into Twelve Step recovery, my faith had gone awry.

More accurately, perhaps, it had burrowed underground. I'd come to think of myself as agnostic simply because I had no other label to apply to my unenlightened estrangement. Fundamentally I believed in God, but my belief had no application—practical or otherwise. In truth, I rarely thought of God. Faith was hardly a subject I wanted to dwell on when I secretly feared it was reserved somehow for others. I'd been living outside the fold for so long that I couldn't imagine there was any way to step inside.

Had anyone asked, I might have confessed that I had no clue how to begin a relationship with God. More likely I would have politely changed the subject—as I'd been doing with my father for years.

That's the point at which I was spiritually stuck the night I attended my first Twelve Step meeting.

* * *

December 3, 1981.

What luck. Did the meeting *have* to be located in a church?

I found it easily enough. Webb's Chapel United Methodist Church was only a stone's throw from my own suburban neighborhood north of Dallas. I'd driven past the church dozens of times.

But now it was more than a landmark. It had taken on a special significance.

I parked near the cluster of cars by the side door and followed the sound of voices down a short hallway to a meeting room where a dozen people clustered around a table. Making room for another chair, they welcomed me as if they'd been waiting for me to show up.

Listening to the words that opened the meeting—a passage from the *Big Book* that I've heard and read thousands of times since—I bristled. The material was sprinkled with references to God.

Was this going to be like one of Dad's visits?

Even with all the talk about God, I knew I needed to hear what these people had to say. I had entered that room in defeat. And it was clear that the men and women there had some kind of solution. Unlike me, they were smiling, calm, apparently content with their lives.

I needed their answer for myself.

I heard I must develop a relationship with a Higher Power in order to recover. Fortunately, I also heard: "We are not saints. The point is, that we are willing to grow along spiritual lines."

Maybe there was hope for me after all.

The ideas I heard that night were transformational. I could "act as if" I had faith. I didn't need to reach some pre-conceived level of piety in order to begin. I could establish a relationship with God right where I was. By praying, I would start to see results, *whether or not I believed.*

Faith could and would grow, if I simply persisted.

It's not uncommon for Twelve Steppers to adopt some goofy concepts of a Higher Power, especially when new. I certainly did. At first I carried my new-found knowledge of God like a treasure tucked in my pocket. My infant faith was something I could pull out, gaze upon, marvel at and tuck away again.

God was my secret.

Prayer was embarrassing for me at that point, even when I was alone. Was this really me, reduced to asking for help? I prayed in an off-handed sort of way, so just in case there really wasn't anyone on the other end listening, I could claim I hadn't really meant it after all. I prayed on the run, jogging in the early morning dark with my Great Dane. I prayed on my feet, in the shower.

I never prayed where I might be seen—not even by my then-new second husband. I *certainly* didn't pray where anyone else might observe me. I wasn't about to invite those condescending smirks I'd seen aimed at outwardly religious people.

For a while I kept my budding relationship with God under wraps.

Then one day God outgrew my pocket. For some reason as I stepped into a local convenience store all I could see were my old favorite substances beckoning like flashing neon on every side. I marched down an aisle lined with temptation to the cooler containing sugar-free, caffeine-free colas. A few minutes later I emerged from the store with my Diet Coke, triumphant.

Something had changed.

Inside the store I'd worn my knowledge of God like a protective cloak, shielding me from my addictions. I'd actually felt enwrapped in his loving care.

This was exciting stuff. *God was growing.* Most important, I was allowing him to grow.

As ludicrous as these statements must seem to someone of lifelong faith or to the more spiritually mature, the recognition of the need for "God growth" is essential for someone who begins in faith like a child.

God is big, *really* big.

How big?

Thiiiis big.

* * *

A few years into recovery I happened upon the J.B. Phillips classic, *Your God is Too Small.* In its descriptions of the ways we can limit our notions of the divine, I recognized some important clues to my human relationships as well.

My former smugness about religious people withered in the light of my own growing belief. I saw how misguided my early thinking had been. I'd been as judgmental of my father and sisters as I'd thought they were of me. I had imagined myself repelled by their faith when I actually feared they had something I needed. I envied them because they possessed something I didn't know how to attain. Ultimately, I realized that Dad and my sisters neither exhibited weakness nor claimed superiority with their faith. Instead, their prayers and their occasional invitations to church events were made out of love for God.

And love for me.

* * *

My father and I have shared some remarkable moments in recent years. One trip brought him to Houston during the sweltering August of 1997 for my first church wedding. Picture the photographs! A fifty-five-year-old bride on the arm of her eighty-two-year-old father, walking down the aisle toward a beloved new husband-to-be.

And toward God.

Today my father is one of my heroes. I want to grow up to be like him in faith.

A few years ago he told me a wonderful story. To keep fit and earn some extra money, Dad works as a janitor for a fast food restaurant. One early morning he encountered a homeless woman in the parking lot near dawn. She wanted to sing a hymn for him. So he listened. When she finished, she asked him to sing a hymn for her. So he did.

When he described this experience to me I was so moved that I knew someday it would find its way into one of my short stories.

For Dad's eighty-fifth birthday, I recorded an audiotape for him—one side with family news, the other with the short story I'd written. It was the best way I could tell him how much I respect his faith and how deeply I share that faith today.

When Dad's phone call came, his voice was thick with

emotion. "I had to call to tell you how much your story touched me," he said.

How amazing. He was thanking *me*.

After our conversation, I sat in silence for some time. I thought of Dad's visit to Dallas years ago and the grueling conversation at my kitchen table. I thought of how many years I had held him at arm's length, resisting all that he represented, while he persisted in loving me and praying for me—whether I wanted him to or not.

And I thought of how long I had distanced myself from God, dreading what I thought he represented, assuming that I could never be worthy, while he continued to love me and watch over me nonetheless.

Abba, father.

Thank you for waiting for me.

Faith Lesson

To rebuild my surrendered life on a faith foundation, I must venture through my dread into the unknown that is God. There I can step into the arms of the heavenly father who has awaited my voluntary return since the moment of my birth.

Course Corrections

═══════════════════════

"I have come to the conclusion that God does not
encourage us to see too far ahead. One simply must accept
the fact that one has no idea where the road one is treading
is going to lead....We like to think that it is terribly
important not to make a mistake ...(but) our mistakes,
if made in good faith, will not result in our being lost....
God often wonderfully weaves mistakes into his plan."
Leslie D. Weatherhead, *The Will of God*

I live southeast of Houston near Galveston Bay where a
dozen small communities cluster around Clear Lake and
NASA's Johnson Space Center. Here, Twelve Step meetings
are liberally sprinkled with oil refinery employees, professional seamen, recreational sailors and people whose careers
have been devoted to the space program.

At one meeting I listened to a retired aerospace engineer
talking about his work with NASA during the Apollo
program. "When we were trying to put men on the moon
we knew that every mission would require some course

corrections," he said. "We never assumed that we had everything perfectly under control from the start."

Contingency planning for trajectory adjustments makes good sense for something so critical as aiming at the moon. Yet Joe wasn't telling his story simply for bragging purposes or entertainment value. Our meeting topic that day was *control*—specifically the futility of trying to control every aspect of our own destinies. Joe's point was that he had finally learned to remain open to course corrections in his personal life, just as he'd learned to do in his aerospace career.

It was a message I need to hear.

* * *

I was twenty-nine years old, married to my first husband, when I took my first college course. In freshman English, as I studied a variety of writers and wrote essays of my own, I knew I'd found my element. My brain re-engaged and for the first time in years I felt hopeful about my own writing.

Soon, with my husband's encouragement, I switched from evening classes to attending school full time. I tackled my education with the same obsessiveness that drove every other aspect of my life in the early '70s. I enrolled in a general honors program which required earning special credits outside my major. And I enrolled in the honors program for English majors.

I'd cherished a dream of becoming a writer from the time I was twelve and had already produced a number of unpublishable short stories, collecting a fat stack of rejection slips along the way. In planning my college work, I aimed for a broad liberal arts education and concentrated my English coursework on the study of literature, to learn what had come before me, rather than on creative writing, my chosen craft. When I was one semester away from my degree, I reaffirmed my original goal by committing to write a short story for my English honors thesis.

I envisioned myself creating a dazzling piece of fiction, impressing my advisor, achieving publication and floating down the aisle to receive my diploma from the University of Maryland in a blaze of glory.

That was my plan.

Here's what happened.

The English professor I most admired, I'll call him Dr. Wilson, didn't have time to serve as advisor for my thesis so he suggested another tenured professor I had never met. Not knowing of anyone else I preferred, I took Dr. Wilson's recommendation.

Portly, balding Dr. Jones slouched indifferently in his office chair during our appointment. He looked more interested in retirement than in my project or a semester-long relationship with me. I discounted his lack of enthusiasm because, after all, it was my story, my honors citation. He'd probably advised countless undergraduates and graduate students over the years, so if he seemed a little burned out, I could see why.

Even so, I felt unsettled as I left his office. We hadn't clicked. I felt no connection. I didn't even *like* Dr. Jones.

I never told anyone about my uneasiness. Certainly not Dr. Wilson. I didn't want to seem ungrateful after he'd taken the time to connect me with a colleague he respected. Besides, Dr. Jones had officially signed on as my advisor. I'd already turned in the signed paper to the English department.

My decision was made.

My direction set.

I simply did what I always did after making a choice ... I followed through.

I began writing and submitting drafts of my short story. Dr. Jones was never in his office when I stopped by, so I left each new revision in his box with a note attached. He never called in response to my notes. And my phone calls went unanswered. Then midway through the semester I learned that his wife had died. So I backed off, not wanting to be a bother to him at such a difficult time.

Meanwhile, I continued revising and polishing my story, bringing it as near as I could to my vision for the work. By the time I submitted my final draft, I fervently hoped I'd written a brilliant piece of fiction. Like many apprentice fiction writers, I was an abysmal judge of my own work, so hope had to serve as a stand-in for a solid grasp of my craft. At semester's end, I shelved my books, caught up on household chores and watched for the mailman. Finally, my grades arrived. Tearing open the envelope I stared at my grades in disbelief. Dr. Jones had given my short story a B!

This wasn't the first B to mar my almost-straight-A record. But this was decidedly worse than the other two. This grade was in my major, my English honors thesis, the culmination of 120 credits of arduous study and work.

I was crushed.

In an uncharacteristically bold move, I phoned Dr. Jones.

Why a B? I asked.

The story deserved a B, he said. It had many good points but wasn't really publishable.

Why didn't you tell me that I was off track? I persisted. I submitted draft after draft and you never said a word.

He figured that Dr. Wilson would point out the problems with the story.

Dr. Wilson? I was dumbfounded. What did Dr. Wilson have to do with it?

After a few more minutes it became clear that Dr. Jones had misunderstood our arrangement from the start. He thought himself my advisor in name only. He'd assumed that Dr. Wilson was working with me on my story.

It was a tough lesson to learn at a perfectionistic point in my life.

There was no changing the B, of course. I had to admit I

deserved it. But I could hardly sidestep my responsibility for the outcome. For an entire semester I'd remained in an uncomfortable situation, getting no help from my advisor but too dogged (or timid) to confront the situation. I'd ignored every sign that our relationship wasn't working, and kept plodding along the path I'd chosen, wearing a yoke that I'd set upon myself.

I had never considered stopping to see if the yoke fit properly.

I had never once considered a course correction.

* * *

My experience with Dr. Jones and my English thesis taught me several things about myself as a person and as a writer. I learned that I must pay attention to my gut reactions and be much more assertive and questioning when I don't feel comfortable with what's going on. I also learned that my college degree didn't automatically render my writing output publishable. I still had a long way to go.

Years later when I arrived in Twelve Step programs, I began to see this experience from a different perspective. Under close examination I discovered I was adamantly resistant to change. But how could that be? I'd always considered myself highly adaptable. Instead I'd often used a claim of "seeing things through" to cover up my aversion to disrupting the current state of affairs. It's amazing how comfortable the familiar can be, even when problematic.

My acquaintance with God in the Twelve Steps introduced me to another way to live—depending on God to guide me, whether I was changing course or embarking on a totally new adventure.

But giving up the illusion of control and learning to live in God's will is an enormous challenge. Twelve Step literature has plenty to say about this subject. The exercise of turning over one's life and will to a Higher Power is the essence of the Third Step. So I continue trying to discern what God's intention might be for my life, and, even more perplexing at times, to allow it to play out in my life.

In his classic work on this subject, Leslie D. Weatherhead asks: "Do I really want to discern God's will, or do I want to get his sanction for my own?" and "Have I got the courage to do God's will when I discern it?"

As often happens to me in recovery, hindsight has proven to be instructive. In my college days I never considered course corrections. That simply wasn't part of my thinking. I paid the price for my grim persistence. Fortunately, I've also learned from the experience.

I've learned that God is the only antidote for fear, allowing me to accept his guidance with varying degrees of courage and serenity.

* * *

I'd been in Twelve Step recovery for several years when I received direction to do something so opposed to my nature that even my sponsor was astonished.

I was leafing through a catalog of continuing education courses at a local college when a voice stopped me. "There," it said. "That's the course you need to take."

Incredulous, I stared at the title: *Certification for Substitute Teachers*.

I laughed aloud. Surely, I was imagining things. I'd never been particularly good with kids and I certainly never considered working as a classroom teacher.

I reached out to turn the page.

"Register for that course." The voice was insistent.

Well, it wouldn't hurt to read the description.

As I did, I realized that the decision to enroll was already made. I couldn't say no. It was already done.

Soon I found myself spending Saturdays getting certified to work as a substitute teacher in my local school district. I supposed that substituting would produce a little income whenever my free lance writing business was flat. But I didn't feel that was the real reason for my being there.

Actually, I couldn't imagine what God had in mind for this crazy adventure.

Neither could my sponsor, Carol A.

"Connie, I don't understand why you're doing this," she would say. "It's just not you at all."

I agreed, but I couldn't *not* do it.

Soon I began to see what God had in mind.

I told Carol A. that I believed God had put me in the classroom and I needed to stick with it until I either grew to like it (questionable) or got over my fear of people.

For some time I'd been aware that my introverted personality was in part a compensation for the inadequacy I felt in relation to others. Now I was humbled to discover how easily I was intimidated by the youthful students. Reminding myself that they had no idea of my insecurities, I forced myself to meet classroom challenges calmly, taking every day of subbing as an opportunity for growth.

I wasn't sure whether high school or middle school was more grueling. The older teens were insufferably rude, ignoring instructions, turning their backs on me to talk with their friends. The kids in middle school were more courteous, but their horseplay kept me ankle deep in spitwads. Every day at school concluded with a pounding headache.

It helped some to know I was there on divine assignment. But whenever I was busy with writing projects, I was ecstatic. That meant I could turn down a call from the school district without guilt and enjoy a day of working in my office at home, in peace.

Finally, after a number of months, just as mysteriously as I received the message to start, I knew when to stop. There was no dramatic epiphany. No audible voice. Just the quiet assurance that it was time, that I'd grown as much as I was likely to grow from my classroom experience.

With a huge sigh of relief I phoned the school district and removed myself from the substitute teacher rolls.

* * *

As you might expect from a newspaper in a city where many eyes are trained on the heavens, the *Houston Chronicle* trumpets every bit of astronomical news. We hear about all the discoveries—planets in neighboring solar systems, comets too dim to be seen before, phenomena that point to the origins of the universe or to the possibility of extraterrestrial life. Of course, the paper carries detailed reports of all NASA flights, including a turn-of-the-millennium shuttle mission that carried astronauts aloft to repair the Hubble Space Telescope.

The astronauts' task included replacing all six of the Hubble's gyroscopes, equipment vital to the telescope's pointing system. The gyroscopes enable astronomers to aim and lock onto distant objects for lengthy observations. They also permit *re*-aiming and *re*-pointing in other directions. Without functioning gyroscopes, the Hubble would continue pointing in one direction, perhaps seeing everything in that field of vision but never seeing what might lie in other directions.

My former attitudes about how I should live my life rendered me as rigidly single-minded as the crippled Hubble with gyros seized up, pointed in one direction, incapable of change even when I felt I'd made a mistake.

In recent years I've been doing some serious goal setting, particularly in relation to my career. But there's a significant difference from years past. Although I plan my plans, and work toward my goals, I try to remain open for guidance.

Today I'm willing to let God maintain my gyroscopes and control my equilibrium, showing me where to direct my attention and energy for my ultimate benefit.

And I expect many course corrections along the way.

Guidance Lesson

A proper relationship with God means I must give up my perceived "right" to control my own life. I must remain ready to realign my plans according to the insight and inspiration that God provides. Through willing adjustments I gain the assurance that I am indeed in the process of transformation, learning to live out God's will for me.

Good Housekeeping

=================================

"The wise have always known that no one can make much
of his life until self-searching becomes a regular habit,
until he is able to admit and accept what he finds,
and until he patiently and persistently tries
to correct what is wrong."
Twelve Steps and Twelve Traditions

I come from a family of obsessive compulsive house-
keepers. I didn't know that while I was growing up.

At my house it was simply the norm that my older sister
Carol and I kept our bedroom looking ready for inspection.
Beds smartly made. Clothes neatly hung or folded away in
dresser drawers. Every book and trinket and hair ribbon in
its place. (No wonder I fit the military lifestyle so easily
when I enlisted in the Air Force at eighteen.) By the time our
little sister Marlyn was five, she was so fastidious about her
room that she cried if playmates left her dolls and toys in
disarray.

My mother inherited her rigorous standards from her

mother. Weekends at my grandparents' house always meant awakening to the drone of Grandma's vacuum. If we slugabed granddaughters were inclined to sleep in past seven, she'd slam open our bedroom door with a cheery, "Rise and shine." Then *whap!* Up flew the window shade. There was dust to chase! A bed to make! Cleaning to do!

From my perspective, the worst part of housecleaning was the end. Usually I'd finished my chores and curled up somewhere with a book by the time the doors and windows were flung open. For a cold-natured kid like me, living in the damp Pacific Northwest, this was miserable. I can still hear the drumming of rain on the roof and the porch, feel the chill breeze whirling through the house. But to Mother and Grandma a proper cleaning wasn't done until everything was rendered spotless, the garbage was taken out and the stale memories of past meals and cigarettes were swept away by fresh, clean air.

For years I assumed that everyone lived like we did. I was grown up before I realized the women in my family were a little over the top.

By then I was one of them.

* * *

Sitting with friends in the student union coffee shop, I listened to Jim describe a project for one of his psychology courses. He was recruiting volunteers for a study, he said, and needed some married subjects. He looked directly at me. It would include a detailed questionnaire and a group discussion. I'd learn a lot about myself, he said. It would be *fun.*

It didn't sound fun to me. It sounded like self analysis and the last thing I wanted to do was to go mucking about in the unknown territory of my psyche.

As a teenager I'd suspected that I was borderline crazy, that my mind might slip its hinges without warning. I had no basis for that belief. But being an introvert I suppose I thought I was unique in having strange, dark thoughts and unpredictable emotions.

I'd long since outgrown the high drama of adolescence. But enough residual anxiety remained that I had no desire at all to delve into myself.

Besides, living with my first husband, I'd grown contemptuous of introspection. He was forever analyzing his life and devising plans for the future. Yet he rarely got around to taking action on any of his insights or decisions.

What was the point of interminable self-examination if it never led anywhere? It appeared to be a colossal waste of time ... as well as scary.

I told Jim I couldn't take part in his psych project. I simply had too much going on to spare the time.

There was a lot of truth in my excuse. I *was* terribly busy in those days.

It takes extraordinary amounts of time and energy to be obsessive. And keeping busy from daybreak to bedtime allows little space for confronting simmering emotions or dealing with any other distressing aspects of life.

* * *

During my enlistment in the Air Force, I had married a career sergeant and we had two children within two years. Although we lived on the opposite coast from my relatives, my family genes kicked in and I kept our home (and our kids) well-scrubbed and sparkling. Every Friday I launched into a thorough vacuuming, dusting, scouring and waxing. Every spring and fall I embarked on a colossal week-long cleaning binge, scrubbing every nook, emptying closets, moving appliances, washing windows and walls, laundering drapes, shampooing carpets. More than once I collapsed into bed at night weeping from exhaustion.

To me a good homemaker was also a good seamstress (like my mother and grandmother). With changing seasons and the onset of each new school year, I bought great mounds of fabric and sewed all Kelly's dresses, all Troy's shirts and countless pairs of pajamas. Long days at the sewing machine and iron were interrupted only by breaks to clean house, prepare meals and handle the intrusions of my family.

During those years even my hobbies got the best of me. A novel or needlework project could keep me up half the night. My stamp collection often trapped me until the wee hours when I'd give in to sleep only with the onset of a headache.

Naturally, I applied the same lack of moderation to my college career. Determined to excel, I studied for astronomy tests as I folded laundry. While cooking I practiced Greek vocabulary and verb conjugations from three-by-five cards taped to the kitchen cupboards. At night I sat at my dining room desk, writing papers for English and history classes while my husband and kids watched TV in the living room.

I earned my degree with several honors citations by attending college year-round for three years.

There should have been a special citation awarded to my family.

* * *

In the years following my graduation in 1975, I divorced, began a career in advertising, remarried and started my own business as a free lance writer. My obsessive behavior shifted from home, school and hobbies to my new career. And to my blossoming addictions.

By the time I found the Twelve Steps in 1981, I knew that my life was out of balance. But I didn't know why or what to do about it. I had no idea that my obsessiveness was a smokescreen, masking a turmoil of emotions and obscuring a deepening concern about the significance of my life. Nor could I see that my compulsive, addictive behaviors blocked me from answers as well.

I never dreamed that the solution would be a thorough housecleaning—a personal, interior housecleaning done in cooperation with God.

I can't say I relished the prospect of self inventory required by the Twelve Steps. Yet I knew my life wasn't working and apparently this process would give me some insight. I sincerely wanted to restructure my life on a foundation of faith, so I trusted that my hopeful new relationship with God would provide the courage I needed for the task.

So I started writing about the past. I wrote about my pride, my fears, my anger, my jealousies, my over-sensitivity. I listed my character defects that had harmed the people around me. I wrote about events large and small that continued to trouble me—some from many years ago. I detailed my relationships with my children, my first husband, my second husband. Every person, event or circumstance of my life that caused me concern went down in my notebook.

Writing as therapy has become common in recent years. But the Twelve Step program expects something more than an emotional dump on paper. I had to discuss my inventory with someone else.

My first sponsor Dorothy was a good listener. She quickly convinced me that I wasn't unique. I hadn't invented any original emotions or taken any actions that someone, somewhere, hadn't felt or done before. She and all my subsequent sponsors—Carol A., Lou, Cindi, Billie, Nancy, Patricia, Nina and Sandra—have helped me see that all my earlier fears about who and what I am were based on ignorance and a misconception of self-sufficiency.

The Twelve Step program is a safe environment for an inward journey—not only because it's made with supportive, non-judgmental friends, but because it's a journey made with God.

* * *

I'm remarkably relaxed about housekeeping today. It's not unusual for me to vacuum and dust only the areas that company will see. I'm able to clean a sink without feeling compelled to scrub the entire bathroom. I can wash a single window without tackling every window in the house. My long-term sponsor Carol A. gave me a priceless gift when she asked, "Don't you realize that you can straighten one drawer without having to clean your whole kitchen?" I'd never considered such a thing.

Just as I learned I could empty and reorganize one closet, I learned that I could clean house internally on specific topics. I wrote one emergency inventory about my tumultuous second marriage. I once scribbled a quick inventory about relationships in the margins of a ballet program. I've written many specialized inventories about my work and my family. Each time I write and share about myself or hear the emotional off-loading of another woman, I experience the fresh wind of a deepening connection with God.

My grandmother died in 1967, my mother in 1986. Sometimes, when I'm missing them, I wonder what sort of women they might they have been, what happiness they might have enjoyed, if they'd had outlets for their emotions besides their mops and vacuums.

They might be surprised at the use I've made of their example.

I'm still dedicated to good housekeeping—the kind that really matters. Today I need little urging to discard the rubbish of my life—whether it's contained in the kitchen trash or in the secret regions of my heart.

Housekeeping Lesson

My spiritual health depends on good stewardship of my

external and internal spaces. I must review my emotions, thoughts and behaviors regularly, accomplishing this task *with* God and *for* God, so he has room to reside in my life, unencumbered by the emotional debris of the past.

Power Struggles

"First of all, we had to quit playing God. It didn't work.
Next, we decided that hereafter in this drama of life,
God was going to be our Director."
Big Book

Dismayed, I let the book fall to my lap.

Was it possible that my husband was right after all?

The night before I'd returned from my first Twelve Step meeting armed with every piece of literature available for sale. I was eager to get on with recovery, to gain some insight into the ideas I'd heard discussed.

Now I'd just read the first sixty pages of *Alcoholics Anonymous*, the *Big Book* I'd been encouraged to buy. A group member had explained that not only AAs but other Twelve Steppers used the *Big Book*. "Addictions are addictions," she said. "We can all relate."

My *Big Book* still wore its industrial-strength blue and white dust jacket. The stiff spine had crackled and complained as the barbed words hit home.

"Any life run on self-will can hardly be a success," I'd just read. "On that basis we are almost always in collision with some thing or somebody, even though our motives are good." If only all the arrangements we made would stay in place, if only the people around us would play their proper roles in the scenarios we created, everything would be wonderful. Wouldn't it?

The *Big Book* didn't stop there. It went on to describe the typical reaction when life didn't go as planned—the firm conviction that other people were to blame. Wasn't such a person "a victim of the delusion that he can wrest satisfaction and happiness out of this world if he only manages well?"

I was skewered.

Granted, the book used different words than I'd been hearing from my husband. But the ideas behind them sounded much too familiar.

I didn't like being challenged on my intentions to improve my marriage. Wasn't love a worthy motive for my words and actions? Worst of all, this annoying book clearly suggested that I was a big part of the reason I collided so often with my husband.

Why was it describing my marital problems anyway?

What did that have to do with my recovery?

* * *

My second husband and I had been married for about a year. We were unquestionably in love, but for reasons that seemed inexplicable at the time, we tangled with distressing regularity. He seemed remarkably closed-minded, ego-driven and quarrelsome. I'd overlooked the hints of these qualities during our brief dating period, but now surely it was my responsibility to show him ways he might get along better with others, including me.

Yet every time I suggested improvements for his relationships with his boss, his sister, his brother-in-law, his best friend, an argument ensued.

Visibly seething, he'd roar that he didn't need to change, didn't want to change and had no intention of changing just because I thought he should.

I was baffled and offended by his unfair accusation. Why, I wasn't trying to do any such thing.

Me? Try to change somebody I loved?

How could he think that of me?

Now here was the *Big Book*, the Twelve Step recovery text, with the audacity to imply that what he said was true.

Was I really fueling our cycle of arguments and reconciliations? Did my husband's angry outbursts actually reflect a truth I'd been unable or unwilling to see?

Ever since we'd met I believed that trying a little harder, a little more lovingly, would eventually convince him to think, feel and act in ways that would lead to his happiness. Then *our* happiness as a couple would be assured.

But the *Big Book* didn't label me a devoted wife for all the energy I'd expended in these efforts. Nothing so affirming as that.

Instead it told me I'd been playing God.

* * *

Change seldom happens overnight. It certainly didn't in my case. But my recognition that morning that I *might* be part of my marital problems, that I might be trying to usurp God's role in my husband's life, was my starting point.

As I attended more meetings I learned that resentments arising from troubled relationships often trigger a return to addictions. And I could see in other members a strong correlation between twisted relationships and a weak or absent relationship with God.

Clearly I hadn't been able to unsnarl my marriage by my

own power.

Since I needed God's help to escape addiction, I supposed I could try him out on my marriage as well. What did I have to lose?

By that time my first sponsor had drifted away from the program and I finally mustered the courage to approach another woman.

At first Carol A. was intimidating. Not that she meant to be. But she had a black-belt, no-days-off approach to recovery, working the program more vigorously than most people I knew. And I'd been listening to her. I'd heard how she turned to God for help with all the tough relationships in her life.

I wanted that kind of recovery. I *needed* it if I were to have any peace in my marriage.

Would she agree to sponsor me?

Soon my routine included daily phone calls to Carol and, with her help, I began to see how I'd been trying to reshape my husband, although I never consciously intended to do so.

Gradually she helped me see that my expectations about marriage weren't all shared by him. He'd come from a West Texas family with traditions and values quite different from my own.

For example, he construed my disagreement with anything he said or believed, as lack of loyalty. For my part, every time we disagreed, I assumed it meant that his viewpoint was *wrong*.

Seeing such facts was a painful, ego-reducing process.

"What did you say *before* the argument started?" Carol would ask me.

Evasive generalities wouldn't work. Only by admitting exactly what I'd said or done was I able to see how I'd set and baited many traps myself.

The pattern was undeniable. I had treated my husband as if I had superior insight with all the correct answers for him

... and for our life together. This dynamic had played out between us in scores of ways.

No wonder he acted as if we were locked in a power struggle.

We were.

Eventually Carol and other women with strong recovery convinced me that my husband was more God's business than mine. They reminded me that I had more than enough to do, just working the Twelve Steps for myself. They said it didn't matter whether my husband had a spiritual program or not. A positive change in our marriage could begin with me—as long as I kept close to God.

That turned out to be far more difficult than I imagined.

*   *   *

I was three or four years into recovery when my husband and I had one of our last major arguments. The reason for the disagreement is long forgotten. The outcome isn't.

But something had set us off that evening and he slammed out of the house into the garage, leaving me smoldering in the kitchen with things unsaid.

By then I knew that he needed time and space alone to cool down after a fight. By then I knew that if I would only pause for a few seconds, God could show me the bigger picture and enable me to behave better than I wanted to.

But I wasn't spiritually grounded that day. All I could see besides dinner simmering on the stove was my own bubbling frustration.

Ego in full bloom, I stomped across the kitchen and grabbed the knob on the garage door.

The door wouldn't open.

Confused, I looked through the window and saw my husband bent over his workbench, ignoring my rattling.

Suddenly I realized what was going on. Sometime since

our last argument he had reversed the doorknob on the door. *He had locked me out of the garage.* Anger mushroomed into rage. *How dare he?*

How could he possibly treat me this way when I was trying so hard to make our marriage work?

In outraged fury I punched my fist through the window.

* * *

The days that followed were one of the lowest points in my recovery.

Life had seemed so much easier when I could blame my moods and reactions on my husband or one of my children. But such evasion techniques wouldn't work any more. Sidestepping responsibility just wasn't acceptable. Not to me. Not to my sponsor. And not to God.

Now that I was trying to live by spiritual principles centered on love, I was dismayed by my tantrum. I knew my behavior wasn't unique. In early recovery many people fall prey to emotional firestorms, acting out feelings in wildly inappropriate ways, even while "getting spiritual." Addictions are excellent mufflers, and giving them up often leaves emotions exposed and raw. It takes some people a long time to build good, new coping skills.

Obviously I had a long way to go.

I needed more recovery.

I needed more God.

* * *

Self disgust is good inducement for change.

By the time my handy husband had replaced the broken window, I'd made a commitment to God and my sponsor that I would abstain from physical violence, just as I abstained from my addictions.

But equally important was my awareness that I didn't want to *act* that way, or even to *feel* that way, ever again.

I no longer wanted to live in a power struggle.

I no longer needed to prove myself right.

No wonder I was worn out. The responsibility for running someone else's life is enormous, particularly when you're resisted every step of the way.

Finally, exhausted, I was ready to place my husband and my marriage in God's hands.

As faith became a working element in my life, my sense of duty about guiding my husband diminished. Freed of the impossible burden of his emotions and actions, I had ample time and energy to take responsibility for my own.

Slowly I began backing up from my old behaviors. I started by reaching for God whenever I was on slippery ground. When I asked for his help, I received the grace to allow my husband time alone after an argument. When I slipped a God thought into a heated discussion, reminding myself of spiritual principles, the tension often diffused before matters escalated to a full-blown conflict. Eventually, I was able to bypass unnecessary confrontations by placing my relationship with God ahead of my ego whenever I sensed a storm brewing.

It's astonishing how swiftly anger diminishes when God is brought into the picture.

Even so, on occasion, my heart would lag behind my actions. At those times I could always apply the prayer a good friend shared with me: "God, you know that I can't love my husband myself today. Please love him for me."

* * *

I've thanked God many times for the lessons of my second marriage. Had it not been for this difficult relationship, I doubt I would have worked the Twelve Step program so diligently. By the time our marriage ended after nearly ten years, we'd both learned much about partnership, and I acknowledged that he too had worked hard trying to make our marriage a success.

But had I not suffered so much from self-inflicted pain, I would never have seen my controlling nature or realized that I must surrender everyone I loved, not just myself, to God.

* * *

Over the years I've bought several copies of the *Big Book* but I still treasure my original. The blue and white dust jacket was replaced long ago with a red leatherette cover. Runaway pages are tacked back in with strips of yellowing tape. The passages that revealed me to myself that long ago morning are marked in black ink, blue ink, red ink, underlined, bracketed and annotated. They bear the coffee stains and grapefruit splatters of countless breakfast readings over the years.

Today when I reread those paragraphs, I'm grateful for the window of grace granted to me in December, 1981, when God enabled me to glimpse a dawning truth and to seek the changes that have affected every relationship in my life in the years since.

Partnership Lesson

When I remember that God is in charge of my earthly relationships it frees me to be a partner to those I love. In this spirit I can live in harmony without scrambling to ensure my emotional security by directing and controlling anyone else's life.

Heavenly Apertures

"Baby, tell me what God is like. I'm starting to forget."
A four-year-old child to her newborn brother
in "Sachi," by Dan Millman
Chicken Soup for the Soul

I've waited too long. So there's no one to blame but myself for the daunting task that lies ahead.

I tap on the door of Mother's little garage apartment. My knock is little more than a courtesy, respect for Mother's privacy, since she remains in bed all the time now. From her bed, which stands in an angle between two windows, she will have seen my car pull up in the driveway. I know she knows I'm here.

Mother's weakened voice calls out for me to come in.

I step inside, wondering if I'm up to this.

When I'd volunteered to write something for Mother's memorial service, my sisters and Mother thought it was a good idea. This would give the minister, who didn't know her well, a way to personalize the service. It would give our family a way to say some final words of love.

Good idea, we said.

But the writing turned out to be harder than I'd expected. I thought it would be a fairly straightforward matter of transcribing the message I'd been carrying around in my heart. Just write it down. Just give it to my sisters for their approval. Just give it to Mother to read. That was the plan. But my procrastination has changed everything.

The increase in Mother's morphine dosage has degraded her vision. She no longer can focus her eyes well enough to read.

I will have to read her eulogy to her.

* * *

Mother moved to Texas only six years earlier. When another serious illness had reminded her of mortality, she arranged a transfer with the giant retailer that employed her and left Anchorage, heading south to be near family. Mother's move placed her, my sisters and me all in one geographical area for the first time in twenty-five years.

There's no doubt in my mind that God inspired our regrouping in the Southwest. (I no longer credit such things to coincidence.) Little did we know then that we'd have such a short time to enjoy having Mother nearby.

When she retired a couple of years after her move, Mother, Carol, Marlyn and I determined to outsmart our busy calendars and the long drives that separated our homes. We planned a regular lunch gathering, choosing a pizza shop near the grade school where Marlyn worked as librarian. There we converged once a month for a grand hour of nonstop conversation, birthday celebrations and just plain fun. Our lunches were often punctuated with gales of laughter over old family jokes and new aging issues. I don't think any of us realized how deeply we'd missed each other until we were all together again.

When Mother became ill, it was no big surprise. She'd been plagued by health problems all her life. But it seemed she knew something was different this time. Hearing that her doctors were running tests for tuberculosis, I sent up a silent prayer for that diagnosis. *Please let it be tuberculosis. There's a cure for TB.*

But soon we learned the somber news. The doctors recommended radiation in hopes of slowing the cancer, of providing Mother some quality time.

She was dying.

Shock is a useful response. I don't recall my immediate feelings. It took some time for me to internalize the significance of the news. Then early one morning reality hit with dizzying force.

I had finished jogging my usual two miles and it was still dark when I stopped to let my dog romp in the field near my house. It was my habit to spend that time in prayer. That morning as I began to pray I was overwhelmed by a sense of helplessness and loss.

How could my life go on without Mother?

The thought wasn't rooted in logic, but in pain. Since I left home at eighteen, I had lived thousands of miles away from my parents. Even growing up, I'd never been overly dependent upon them. But neither of those facts produced any comfort or relieved the sorrow of the moment. For a short time that morning, I was a small child again ... a little girl losing her mother.

* * *

Like most people in their forties, I wasn't unfamiliar with death. All four of my grandparents were gone and I had lost several aunts and uncles. However, living on the opposite coast when most of those deaths occurred and being focused on my immediate family and my self-centered concerns, I'd always been able to maintain an emotional as well as physical distance.

So death wasn't a stranger to me. But I'd never really handled it. Not until 1979. Not until Tom.

A short time before Mother moved to Texas, when I was between my first and second marriages, I met an exceptional man and fell in love. Almost overnight my entire life changed. We'd even begun to talk of marriage.

Then one bright summer morning in my office at a Dallas advertising agency, something incredible happened. I was wrestling with the words for a magazine ad when I decided I needed a stretch break. As I stood up from my desk I noticed the clock above my cubicle wall. Eleven-thirty A.M.

Suddenly arms encircled me from behind my back. The embrace was so warm that I knew it was Tom, the love so intense that it almost took my breath away. I reached up to touch his arms and turned my head to see him, but the sensation and the presence were gone.

Except for me, my office was empty. Tom wasn't there. No one was there.

Distracted by the strange occurrence, I went back to my work.

At home that evening I wasn't thinking at all about the mysterious embrace as I dialed the number for Tom's home. An unfamiliar voice answered the phone so I identified myself as a friend.

The man on the other end of the line told me he was Tom's brother. "Tom died this morning," he said. "He was pulling onto the highway near his house when a truck hit his van. He was killed instantly."

Somehow I ended the call and hung up the phone.

Somehow I made it through that evening, that night.

Somehow I made it through the next days and weeks.

Tom had died at 11:30 A.M. on June 6. That much, everyone knew. But I was the only one who knew Tom had stopped by my office afterward to say goodbye before he moved on.

In those days, I wasn't in the habit of turning to God. (This happened two years before my introduction to the Twelve Steps.) But awed by the anguish of grief, I prayed anyway. Maybe my early childhood training in "Now I lay me down to sleep" kicked in. Perhaps some deep instinct took over. But in some primitive way I knew that the cries of my heart reached their destination.

It was no stretch at all for me to envision Tom in another dimension. I simply knew he was with God. And I knew he and God could hear every word that I said.

Even more significantly the separation between *here* and *there* seemed almost negligible. The zone where God and Tom existed seemed merely a breath away.

* * *

After radiation treatments, Mother rallied briefly during the summer months before slipping into her final decline.

This was totally different from my experience with Tom. At the same time I braced for the pain of Mother's death, I dealt with the daily sorrow of a gradual loss. I prayed hard and often. Over the weeks and months my prayers matured as I asked for the insight and courage to support Mother in her illness and for the wisdom and strength to be of comfort to other members of the family.

Mother's cancer thrust me into a whole new phase of faith development.

This doesn't mean that all went smoothly.

In November, Mother, Carol, Marlyn and I welcomed a funeral director to her little house for consultation. We all seemed quite rational as we discussed the process and the cost of picking up Mother's body and conducting her cremation. The young man seemed a bit unnerved by our composure and good humor. Actually our laughter must have unnerved us too. The funeral director had barely driven away when our taut emotions erupted sideways in a stinging four-way argument over something trivial.

We'd settled the *how* of her dying. But that left the unanswerable question of *when*.

By November Mother had wrapped up her simple financial matters and distributed most of her belongings. Everything that remained was listed with the name of the daughter, son-in-law or grandchild who was to receive each item.

She was ready. What's more, she was at peace about leaving.

She had already heard the angels.

"I heard a choir singing," she said one day, pointing out her window into the far north. "Way up there." Mother had never been outwardly religious, not even a nominal churchgoer. But if her faith were ever in question, the look on her face erased any doubt. And beneath her words I could hear how much she needed to know we believed.

"It was the most beautiful music I've ever heard," she said. "Didn't you hear it?"

No. None of us had heard it.

It wasn't our time.

It wasn't our choir.

Obviously God and Mother were handling some private business that had nothing to do with me or anyone else around her. This was a serious matter—something between the two of them.

My sisters and I thought maybe Mother's passing might be her gift from God on Thanksgiving. Then maybe for her December fifteenth birthday. Christmas, perhaps? New Years?

* * *

Mother sits up in bed and puts her legs over the side so that I can sit beside her. She wears one of her pastel flowered cotton nightgowns. Always petite, she's now gaunt, her arms and hands impossibly frail. Her chest rises and falls with the increasing effort of her breaths.

Sitting with her on the side of her bed, I stall a little. I tell her that Carol and Marlyn have both read the eulogy.

"Good," she says.

We're all of one accord. We agree that it says what we want to say.

"Good," she says.

Finally, there are only the words on the page.

Beside me, Mother waits.

I look at the few paragraphs on the single typed sheet of paper in my lap. Have I been praying to God for courage all these months for nothing?

I take a deep breath and begin.

Her attention feels like a gift.

In turn I give her the only gift I can imagine she could want right now—reaffirmation of the family's love, assurance that we're ready to release her to what comes next.

"That's very nice," she says when I'm done. "Thank you."

The moment feels strange, anti-climactic. Her little house is silent as I help her back into bed.

Mother feels distant, as if she's already slipping away, as if she already belongs somewhere else, as if she's listening again for her angels, drawing near.

* * *

My children are in their mid-thirties today. While I think back to their births I remember a sentimental wallow in motherly hormones—my healthy babies delighted me—but I don't remember thanking God. That's how irrelevant he was to me in those days.

By the time I made the acquaintance of the Romantic poets in college, I'd grown a bit wiser, or perhaps just less shallow. I instantly recognized the meaning of Wordsworth's lines: "trailing clouds of glory do we come / from God, who is our home ..." Although I didn't allow God into my life then, I could still perceive the truth when it demanded little more of me than appreciation for a fine·turn of phrase.

What would giving birth be like for me now? I wonder. (Not that I care to be a modern day Sarah. But I'm curious, after all.) Would I do birth differently? Would I experience it with the exquisite sense of God's nearness that captivates me now in middle age?

Would I see through the portal as I did with Mother? With Tom? With my father-in-law Fred as I prayed by his bedside moments after he died?

As I write these words, several friends are expecting babies. One is Donna, a special friend of more than ten years. As I watch her move through her pregnancy, I have a twinge of envy. Donna has the chance to do it right. She has the chance to bear her child with God. To peer through the aperture for a hair's-breadth of an instant.

"Don't miss it," I must tell her. "Don't miss it."

* * *

Recently I dreamed of Mother.

The setting was ambiguous, hazy. But she was whole and healthy, vivid and real as we walked toward each other. I knew I was dreaming and, given the way that dreams often play out, I expected her to disappear or for the scene to shift before I could touch her.

Yet everything in me longed to feel her arms around me once again.

Smiling, we drew closer. We stretched out our arms and, blessing of blessings, we embraced.

For a long moment I experienced my mother again, as intensely as that winter day years ago when I sat beside her in her little house, reading her eulogy.

I was still enveloped in her love as I awoke.

I recorded the date of that dream in the margin of a favorite meditation book. I wanted a lasting reminder of this extraordinary gift, an ephemeral moment when a delicate membrane opened between here and there, when God granted me an inestimable treasure, spilling into my subconscious the precious essence of my mother's love.

Passage Lesson

I believe that I'm a brief sojourner in life, dipping down from a greater reality into this temporary earthly realm. If I'm alert, if I draw near as others negotiate their incomings and outgoings, I may not only be of service to them, but may glimpse the reality of God that normally lies far beyond my comprehension and reach.

Keeping Score

"...Out of every season of grief or suffering, when the hand
of God seemed heavy or even unjust, new lessons for
living were learned, new resources of courage were
uncovered, and ... finally, inescapably, the conviction
came that God *does* 'move in a mysterious way
His wonders to perform.'"
Twelve Steps and Twelve Traditions

"Mother, we have to stop."

Grimly I kept my eyes on the road.

We were driving through rolling, wooded, spring-green
countryside that challenged the popular image of prairie-dry
Texas. After a shower the sunshine contrasted sharply with
my dark emotions.

It hadn't been a good day. And now this.

"Mother, we can't just leave that poor puppy out here,"
Kelly persisted.

Frustrated, torn with indecision, I lifted my foot from the
accelerator and the speedometer needle began creeping down.

The last thing either of us needed was another pet. I had a Great Dane and three cats at home. Kelly shared her apartment with a high-maintenance Irish setter. What would either of us do with the skinny tan pup we'd seen nosing through the rain-damp weeds on the roadside?

We were on our way home to Dallas after visiting Troy. I hadn't seen my son for more than six months. Six months of prayer. Six months of talks with my sponsor to get fortified against an emotional meltdown.

I'd thought I was ready. I *hadn't* fallen apart. But the visit had been agonizing.

I was grateful for Kelly's company on the drive home. She was far more objective about our family turmoil than I. As a mother, I was enmeshed in the pain of watching a grown child suffer—an adult who was clearly beyond my guidance and control.

I was in no mood for the added complication of a stray animal.

If I'd been alone I might have kept driving. I might have told myself that someone else would stop to help the little dog. I might have convinced myself that I just imagined the protrusion of the puppy's ribs, his single-minded search for something edible among the weeds, the stiff hind legs that dragged along behind him.

But Kelly's determination and my own better nature won out.

With a sigh, I pulled the car to the side of the road, waited for a break in traffic and circled back to retrace the last half-mile.

* * *

It hadn't been a good day.

In fact, it hadn't been a good year.

My mother had died in January after a ten-month battle

with cancer. After her death, as I worked through my grief, more and more of my attention was free to refocus on my son. How I wanted to solve his problems. How I wanted him to succeed in life.

Finally, to reclaim my sanity and restore balance in my own life, I turned to a Twelve Step program that taught the principle of detachment with love. I'm not sure which of us my tough love was harder on—Troy or me.

After Troy left Dallas the anguish of reading his letters was so intense that I'd began calling my sponsor before I opened them, reading them to her so we could deal with my reactions together, right then, over the phone.

Carol A. had more years in recovery than I, more experience in depending on God. She'd also worked her way through troubled periods in each of her children's lives. "Rescue is robbery," she said to me over and over. "When you save your grown children from the consequences of their choices, you rob them of the opportunity to learn from their mistakes and to grow up."

At great cost I was developing a strong program of my own, based on the conviction that Troy was a beloved child of God.

For now, that had to be enough.

For now, I had to be at peace with that knowledge, even though I knew my son wasn't in touch with the truth of God's assurance for himself.

* * *

To my surprise the puppy came instantly when I called. Trusting. Front legs trotting. Hind-quarters hip-hopping along. Tail wagging behind.

I could see the ticks from a distance of five or six feet.

Groaning, I opened the trunk of the car. This was hardly the kind of roadside emergency I envisioned when I'd placed an extra can of oil, a flashlight, and a towel in my trunk. But it would do. I made a pallet with the towel and gingerly lifted the puppy, trying to avoid touching the bloated black insects.

As I placed the little dog in the trunk, he laid down on the towel and looked up at me with an expression I could only read as gratitude. I assured him we wouldn't dawdle along the way and closed the lid.

Starting the engine, I looked at Kelly.

Now what? I wondered as I pulled the car back onto the highway for the hour's journey to Dallas.

* * *

My husband was home from work by the time Kelly and I pulled into the driveway. We took the puppy from the car into the garage and the three of us mixed up a noxious bucket of flea and tick dip and bathed away the pup's load of parasites.

We dried him, praised him and set him before a feast.

Even well-fed dogs are lusty eaters. But the slurping and smacking of that puppy over his bowl of Purina Dog Chow probably reached all the way to heaven.

After Kelly went home that evening, my husband and I agreed that the puppy could live in our fenced back yard. For a little while. As long as it got along with our Great Dane and our cats who had free access to the yard through a pet door. Just until we decided what to do.

Over the next two days I tried to keep an emotional distance. Through the picture window in our den, I watched the pup survey his new domain, barking at playful squirrels in the pear tree and neighbors' voices beyond our fence.

In spite of myself a bond developed over countless bowls of moistened kibble.

By the third day, I told my husband I would like to keep

the puppy. He agreed.

I made an appointment with the vet.

* * *

The next afternoon I hung up the phone heartsick.

Our veterinarian, who'd asked me to leave the pup with him for a few hours, had taken his x-rays and come to his conclusion. The puppy's crippled legs were due to an old injury. He was probably struck by a car. At any rate, the injury had healed badly—very badly—and it was inoperable. The puppy's hind legs would never work properly.

But he gets around all right, I said.

Yes, came the reply, but he'll always be in pain.

I took the recommendation of my trusted vet and made the decision to euthanize.

For days I cried at the most unexpected times. On the phone with Carol A. each morning, I talked about the puppy.

Finally she said, "I know you're sad, Connie, but I don't think the puppy is what this is all about. I think there's something else you're not looking at."

I couldn't make the connection instantly. It might have been days or perhaps a week before I saw the truth. When I did, it was so obvious I couldn't imagine how I'd failed to see it.

The crippled puppy had become a substitute for my son, whose life I could neither change nor mend. I had enfolded the puppy into my heart as if he were divinely bestowed, a new part of God's plan for me.

But things hadn't turned out the way I'd expected.

I was denied the puppy as Troy's replacement.

Now I had two sorrows instead of one.

* * *

Sad as it was, the insight helped to drain some power from my emotions. I felt as if I were moving ahead, living in recovery once again.

Surely God was looking on with approval at how well I was doing.

But three months later I was back in my veterinarian's office. This time the patient was my nine-year-old Russian blue cat. Spook had lost a kidney a short time earlier due to kidney stones. Now her remaining kidney was shutting down.

It's only a matter of time, said the vet. The kindest thing to do ....

His eyes reflected the sorrow I felt. He'd worked long and faithfully trying to save this little cat.

I went home that day, bereft.

* * *

During the weeks that followed I tried to draw clarity from confusion.

From my earliest days in recovery I'd scorned a belief in a punishing God who kept a tally of wrongs. But somewhere along the way I'd made a subtle and insidious shift in thinking. I'd been living as if God were keeping score, not of my failings, but of my achievements—the strides I made in my program, my devotion to building a spiritual life.

At a subconscious level I thought I deserved a reward.

Surely, since I'd handled Mother's death so well ...

Surely since I was striving so hard in my marriage ...

Surely since I was working on my relationship with Troy ...

Surely since I was denied the crippled puppy ....

Surely, after all that, God would allow Spook to recover. One cat was a small thing to ask in return for working my program so well, for being so good.

But God hadn't been keeping score.

I had.

The hardest thing to accept in life can be a resounding celestial silence.

Scorekeeping Lesson

God's grace is a given, but my embracing that grace doesn't necessarily mean my life will be comfortable. If I expect to earn compensation here on earth I'm doomed to disappointment. My spiritual growth must be the ultimate measure of life well lived. And the joys I experience along that rugged path must be sufficient reward.

Slipping the Trap

"When I have met an immigrant tottering under a bundle
which contained his all ... I have pitied him, not because
that was his all, but because he had all *that* to carry ....
If I have got to drag my trap, I will take care that it be a
light one and do not nip me in a vital part."
Henry David Thoreau
Walden

Something strange was going on at my house, and the
phenomenon centered in my office. A corner bedroom with
two windows, my office was the brightest room in the house.
But in recent months the atmosphere had grown thick and
oppressive. Every morning when I closed the door, set my
coffee on the desk and settled down to work, I felt a mount-
ing uneasiness as if something were pressing in on me.

Looking for the source of the problem I didn't see anything
particularly new or different. There were some new books, but
there were *always* new books. Nothing unusual in that.

My office was lined with half a dozen seven-foot-tall

walnut bookcases that loomed over me as I worked. Volumes stuffed every shelf. Books stood upright. Books lay cross-wise to fill the gaps. Books spilled out into stacks on my desk and file cabinets. Books teetered in piles on the floor.

Leaving my office to refill my coffee mug, I passed more books. The headboard in the bedroom was crammed to over-flowing. Books lay on the coffee table and end tables in the living room. Books stood in shelves in the den. Books cluttered the pass-through counter between the dining room and the kitchen.

All my life I'd harbored a fantasy of living in a library. (If heaven is our heart's desire, mine would be a gigantic library.) To be surrounded by books—all the wisdom ever recorded right at my fingertips—ah, what could be more satisfying? My vision had a practical side as well. It included endless leisure for reading, studying, learning.

Well, the last part hadn't materialized. There was work to do, money to earn, a life to live. But other than that, I was virtually living my dream.

Why wasn't I ecstatic?

Surely my cherished books couldn't be the problem.

I cast a critical look over the shelves. Dozens of reference books supported my work as a writer. And the fiction ... well, I just loved fiction. But there were also plenty of volumes I intended never to open again—like my college algebra text, an outdated book on anthropology, some screamingly dull monographs from a disappointing archeology course.

I'd made two household moves since graduating from college, but it had never occurred to me to get rid of any textbooks. What self-respecting booklover would do such a thing?

* * *

When I was growing up my sister Carol and I played

library. With Mother's permission we would lug all her book club novels and all her navy bound, gold-titled classics upstairs to our bedroom. We'd line them up with our own books and take turns being librarian, checking them out, checking them in. (Today Carol's treasured keepsakes include a Golden Book with one of our homemade library card pockets pasted inside the cover. Ironically, it was Marlyn, the pesky little sister we excluded from our play, who grew up to become a librarian.)

By the time we outgrew our makeshift bedroom library, I was regularly using a *real* library card and reading my way through Mother's books. In my teens when I earned money of my own, my personal library began to grow, expanding with every stage of my life. High school: *The Complete Works of Shakespeare, The Complete Sherlock Holmes.* My enlistment in the Air Force: *The History of Flight.* My first marriage: the Time-Life Series *Great Ages of Man,* the *Encyclopedia Britannica.* Then my journey through four years of college.

In one of my first literature courses I met that eccentric American Henry David Thoreau who plunged into the woods to test his mettle and his philosophy of life. His determination to strip life to its essentials fascinated me. From the perspective of a spartan existence, he painted a vivid picture of people so fixated on possessions that they labor through life "dragging their traps behind them." Thoreau even went so far as to claim that the fox in Aesop's fable was lucky to leave behind his extraneous tail when he escaped a trap. "No wonder man has lost his elasticity," he scolds. "It would surpass the powers of a well man nowadays to take up his bed and walk."

In college I found Thoreau's quaint intensity a little amusing. But even then I must have sensed a message for me in his experience because the image of a trap became snagged in my mind like a bit of cloth in brambles. Nearly ten years later I was ready for his counsel.

Insidiously, over years, books had assumed an importance in my life far beyond my love for reading. They were out of control. Their sheer weight and presence had become an obstruction. Instead of producing joy, they were troubling the peace of my home, muddling my mind and choking up my channel to God.

There was no denying that my office, my home, spoke for me. Books were my idol. In spite of my Twelve Step recovery, in spite of my growing faith, I was still clinging to a false god.

Given that awareness there was only one thing I could do.

That same afternoon I gathered up some cartons and sturdy paper sacks and set to work. Shelf by shelf, bookcase by bookcase, I proceeded through my office and the rest of the house. By the time I finished my task, I'd loaded my car with eighteen bags and boxes of books.

The local used book store paid a paltry sum—about five dollars, I recall—for the entire batch. I should have paid *them* for the service they rendered to my soul.

At home I walked through my house with a sense of wonder. Every book now had a place on a shelf. There were even some empty spaces.

The gravity in the house was reduced.

I could *breathe.*

I could *think.*

I felt spiritually open once again.

The message was clear. God knew I was placing entirely too much value on my books. And he wasn't content—nor was I—until I'd given up some of my treasures so I might establish a stronger connection with him.

* * *

In the months following my great off-loading of books,

other insights suggested that the issue ran far deeper. Books were simply the most obvious manifestation of my entire approach to life.

Taking stock of my home, I realized that I'd always gravitated to heavy, dark, substantial furniture. I decorated with warm colors, earthtone accents. I chose window coverings thick enough to shut out the first hint of darkness or gloom.

I went to great lengths to create a cozy haven.

It was essential that my home feel safe and secure.

And I surrounded myself with possessions. A collector since the age of ten when my first boyfriend introduced me to stamp collecting, I'd added collections of glass paperweights, rocks and minerals as an adult. (Naturally, each collection required a shelf or two or three of related books.) My collections were modest in value—I was never a big spender—but I'd found something satisfying, reassuring, about making new acquisitions. And my collections often grew with less attention to quality than to quantity.

A friend once told me that she regularly discarded anything that she hadn't used in two years. What a frightening policy! I doubted that I needed to go as far as she did to achieve personal balance (she didn't even have photographs of herself that predated her Twelve Step recovery), but I *did* need to examine my tenacious connection to things.

Materialistic?

Me?

To me materialism meant big-ticket items like lavish homes, boats, clothes and expensive cars. But was my five- and ten-dollar grasping any less reproachable?

The question made me cringe.

So did my answer.

My particular brand of materialism wasn't driven by greed or competition. Mine was driven by fear.

Everything about my behavior over the years testified to a scramble for emotional security. My cozy nest with all my books and collections fixed me in place. It provided assurance of my place and value in the world—an assurance that I shouldn't need ... not if I were truly relying on God.

"We trust infinite God rather than our finite selves," the *Big Book* says. Those words came back to me as I evaluated my style of living. And I heard a depth of truth in that statement that I'd never understood before.

Only by relying on God for my earthly security, would I ever be truly free.

* * *

I still own a few hundred books. My husband Pete has capitulated to the library look as baskets and boxes and shelves of books have infiltrated our household as part of the decor. There's a handy bookcase beside our dining room table where we do our spiritual reading in the morning. There's a bookcase in the guestroom for wakeful visitors. And as I write this, I'm considering a bookcase for the master bedroom to handle the overflow from the headboard of our bed.

But today there are major differences.

Last year we completed a renovation of my office and a major part of that project was another great book purge. Gone are the heavy, dark bookcases and the walnut-topped black desk that had followed me from my old life. Now in their place stand white bookcases against off-white walls. From my new, washed oak desk I have a view through glass doors across the rolling backyard of our townhome community to Clear Lake. Today I work in physical brightness that encourages spiritual buoyancy.

Today books no longer possess me. Nowadays I let them pass through my life. I can load up books for recycling at the bookstore without a twinge of remorse. I lend books to friends without agonizing over the odds of their return.

I've also noticed with interest that as my spiritual life increases, my obsession with my collections declines. I seldom add to my collections anymore and when I do I no longer seek the adrenaline rush of acquisition, but the quiet pleasure in the artistry or natural beauty of a new purchase.

A purist like Thoreau would surely contend that I still drag a sizeable trap behind me. And I suppose it's true. But I know that as long as I focus on God and avoid the seductive lure of false security, my worldly trap will remain harmless, unarmed, unable to "nip me in a vital part."

Security Lesson

If I look to earthly things for my sense of self or my security in this world, God will shake that flimsy structure until I'm forced to readjust my view and fix my sights on him.

Wholly, Holey, Holy

"Holiness consists not in a cowl or in a garment of gray.
When God purifies the heart by faith, the market
is sacred as well as the sanctuary;
neither remains there any work
or place which is profane."
Martin Luther

The weather was abysmal that January day as Kathy and I worked our way north on Interstate 35, returning home to Dallas from an out-of-town writers conference. Her windshield wipers struggled to stay ahead of the freezing rain and we were both relieved when we escaped the wintry onslaught near the outskirts of the city.

Relaxing with the improvement in weather, we visited and compared notes about the conference as Kathy drove a route into east Dallas that I'd never traveled before. Suddenly we rounded a curve and I spotted a freight train on the horizon. My friend chatted on, oblivious to what lay ahead. Her foot never left the gas pedal and we began to close the distance rapidly.

Finally, I could stand the tension no longer. "Kathy," I blurted, "the train!"

Startled, she glanced at me and laughed. "Oh. Don't worry. Watch."

Don't worry? Watch for what? I sat frozen to my seat as we hurtled toward the stream of rocking freight cars. A few seconds later we topped a crest in the road and I saw why Kathy chuckled. A quarter of a mile ahead, the road dipped into an underpass that carried us beneath the thundering freight train and safely on our way.

* * *

My experience with Kathy and the freight train years ago taught me a useful lesson about perspective.

To borrow a term from another transportation industry, I've learned that what I discern may not match the *mental model* of others. In aviation, pilot training emphasizes the importance of situational awareness and of communicating with other crew members so everyone on the flight deck has the same understanding of where they are, where they're going and what it will take to get there.

That wintry day in Dallas Kathy and I hardly shared the same mental model as we sped toward a train. She had the accurate picture. My image of reality was totally skewed by what I *thought* I saw.

What I think I see, what I think I hear, what I think I understand aren't always the way things really are. And it's not only a confusion about surroundings that contribute to my misperceptions. Sometimes it's simply a misinterpretation of words.

* * *

I was once in the midst of a pleasant conversation with a

friend when he turned stiff, sullen and unresponsive for no apparent reason. After a few minutes I asked him what had happened to change his mood.

"I don't appreciate being insulted," he said.

I'm sure my mouth fell open. I'd just told him how much I admired his easy relationships with people. How on earth had that caused an affront?

It took a few minutes and several more questions before I discovered he had misunderstood a word. Confusing *gregarious* with *garrulous*, he thought I'd accused him of talking too much.

Happily we were able to clear up the matter, laugh about it and go on.

I could relate to my friend's defensiveness however. My own misinterpretations about certain religious words had served as an obstacle to my relationship with God for years.

* * *

Holy is a four-letter word at many Twelve Step meetings.

If someone's sharing comes across as "too religious" for the comfort level of the group, somebody's likely to grumble: "I didn't come here to get holy. I came here to get *well.*"

Typically other heads around the room bob in agreement. *Don't preach to me,* is the unstated message. *This is a spiritual program not a religious program, and I get all the God I need right here, thank you.*

I felt the same way in my early days of recovery. For a while it was all I could do to learn the Twelve Step vocabulary of addiction and recovery—words like surrender, insanity, powerlessness, willingness, moral inventory, character defect, humility, amends, carrying the message.

Eventually I began learning a faith vocabulary too. At first even basic words such as *God* and *prayer* felt alien to my tongue. I was hardly ready for anything more advanced. But

I could see that if I wanted to change it would take a conscious effort to break down the barrier of negatively charged words that stood in my way—the kind of words that resounded with dogma, doctrine, liturgy, solemn robes, judgmentalism ... *church*.

Words like *holy* in those religion-resistant days had one connotation for me: "holier than thou."

But as I studied Twelve Step literature, I concentrated on reading with my heart, attempting to bring in new spiritual ideas at a level below my mind. Such concepts, I learned, were more likely to find fertile ground in my heart than in my intellect. Gradually, the words surrounding God grew less forbidding.

* * *

In time, I swung to another extreme, puffed up with self-congratulations about my spiritual progress. When I discovered the St. Francis Prayer in Step Eleven of *Twelve Steps and Twelve Traditions*, I quickly adopted it as the centerpost of my daily devotions. One day I was carrying on at great length to my friend Gisela, telling how this prayer was changing me, how the emphasis on love, forgiveness, understanding and self-forgetting was helping me grow in humility, how some of the worst aspects of my ego were slipping away.

Then I realized Gisela had been shaking her head, frowning, throughout my monologue.

"Not me," she said. "I can't use that prayer at all."

Dumfounded, I asked her why not.

She described her rigid, unforgiving Catholic upbringing. To her the St. Francis Prayer was simply one more piece of religious oppression, directing her not just to live in God's will, but in subservience to everyone around her.

Same prayer. Totally different messages.

Time and an open mind can do wonders—along with a

few well-placed nudges from God. Eventually I saw just how little I really knew and began to taste *real* humility.

Eventually Gisela learned to read with her heart. Today she loves and uses the St. Francis Prayer as readily as I do in our shared quest for more God-directed lives.

* * *

Of the ten definitions my hefty Random House dictionary offers for the word *holy*, I like this one best: *dedicated or devoted to the service of God.*

Simple. Sweet. Challenging.

In my pre-Twelve Step days I was proud of my compartmentalized lifestyle. I was one woman at work. Another with my family. Still another in social settings. But once I was in recovery this segmentation no longer worked.

As I developed a life orientation grounded in faith, I realized that everything about me—my relationships, my career, every dream and desire—must be opened up for God's healing energy and transforming power. I no longer wanted to live as a fragmented person, with selected parts of me hidden away.

I began to see the value and simplicity of a unified life, one cut from a single piece of cloth. Gradually my words, attitudes and behaviors grew more uniform, more true to the person I was becoming.

The *Big Book* says: "We claim spiritual progress rather than spiritual perfection," yet the Twelve Steps have never excused me from diligently pursuing a high ideal. And although the character defects that have bedeviled my recovery are an inescapable part of being human, I can continue to release those flaws as I aim for a more positive, *more holy*, life.

* * *

Some years ago I attended a ten-day writers conference in Port Townsend, Washington, where I reveled in the mild Pacific Northwest summer, the challenge of inspiring speakers and workshops, and the companionship of a small group of new friends whom I met through my announcement of a daily Twelve Step meeting.

During an evening reading of fiction and poetry, one of these friends, an elegant middle-aged woman, mesmerized the audience by reciting a poem about her surrender and recovery. The title of her poem: "Wildly Imperfect."

Yes! That's exactly how it is.

And exactly how I am.

Wildly imperfect. Totally human. Wholly, holey, holy.

Striving to live a unified life, one unswervingly pointed toward God.

Vocabulary Lesson

I grow in faith by reflecting on words and ideas that were off-putting in my God-shunning days and by incorporating their meaning into my life. Today I can embrace holiness as a personal ideal—even while I acknowledge my blemishes and shortfalls as a human being—reaching toward the perfection I believe God envisions for me.

The Intruder

"It must be understood that (my) conversion...was only to
Theism, pure and simple, not to Christianity.... I now
number it among my greatest mercies that I was permitted
for several months, perhaps for a year, to know God and to
attempt obedience without even raising that question...."

C.S. Lewis
Surprised by Joy

I didn't know what hit me that morning.

I had eaten my breakfast cereal and fruit, finished my cus-
tomary reading in the *Big Book* and other Twelve Step materials and remained at the table where I closed my eyes for a
period of quiet. I had recently added a new discipline, meditation, into my daily routine. Typically I devoted only a few
minutes to the effort, but even so I wasn't finding it easy.

That morning as I stepped into the usual place for my meeting with God—a clearing in a wood with a rushing mountain
stream—something curious happened.

Before I could begin my solitary approach to God, I saw

someone else in the clearing. Someone in human form.

A celestial gate-crasher.

Unexpected and uninvited, he stepped forward to welcome me *into my own meditation.*

Recoiling, I bounced back out of my envisioned space, back to the chair at the kitchen table surrounded by my books and breakfast dishes.

Who was this intruder?

Even as I voiced the question, I tried to dodge the answer. Off balance and annoyed, I grumbled to myself that I just wasn't ready for this.

I wasn't ready for *this* at all.

* * *

Prayer had been a relatively easy new habit for me to incorporate into my Twelve Step recovery. After several years I'd established a predictable routine—prayers first thing in the morning, last thing at night and before each meal, plus an occasional urgent appeal when I was in an emotional snarl. In retrospect, I'm sure that many of my petitions were rushed and superficial. Nonetheless, prayer had been retraining my secular mindset, pointing my thoughts more consistently toward God. Without a doubt, prayer had begun to change me, softening me at a subconscious level.

Still, I wasn't content with my routine. I knew I was skirting an important part of the recovery program by neglecting meditation.

"Just sit quietly and empty your mind," people advised in meetings where meditation was the topic. But after numerous attempts to stop my churning thoughts, I counted myself a dismal failure.

Then I heard someone say that he read the *Big Book* and the *Twelve and Twelve* every morning, putting God ideas in the place of his old thinking. He considered that his meditation.

I can do *that*, I told myself. In fact, I was already doing it, spending time with recovery literature every day. I could simply give my morning reading a new label, which I did. For the next couple of years I followed the "reading method" of approaching God.

All this reading had distinct benefits but, being miles away from the spiritually recognized method of *lectio divina*, it was a poor excuse for mediation. Unquestionably I grew in head knowledge. But, evading the real challenge, I made minimal progress in any experiential knowledge of God.

Finally I heard a bit of practical wisdom from a friend, Ruth, who described her meditation method, saying. "I imagine myself in a clearing in the woods. That's where I go to spend time with God every day."

Borrowing Ruth's image, I dressed it up with some custom touches. I added a sparkling stream chattering over a rocky course like the mountain rivers I remembered from the Pacific Northwest. I envisioned a log near the riverbank. God, a nebulous figure, sat with his back to me, facing the tumbling river.

Many Twelve Steppers are encouraged to define what they want "their God" to be. This seems a useful exercise for some. But everything in me rebelled at any attempt to impose human definition or limitations upon God. I needed a creator who was far greater than anything my feeble imagination could devise.

So I was content, at least for the time being, with a vague image. Each morning I approached this fuzzy notion of God with the intention of just *being* with him.

A flimsy meditation perhaps. But an honest attempt. And it seemed to be working—that is, until the intruder appeared.

* * *

Kelly and I were both a little shocked at the vehemence of

my reaction the evening she called to invite me to a mid-week service at her church.

Not just *no*.

But, *NO!*

Ironically my daughter had found her own way to religion. As a young adult, living alone, she'd discovered her spiritual needs and found a place to be fed. Since she knew I'd embraced God through my Twelve Step programs, she apparently thought I'd be receptive to attending a worship service.

Nothing could have been further from the truth.

In my unchurched arrogance I disapproved of the church Kelly attended. Enormous, aggressively evangelical, it had a high-profile television ministry and a high-income, highly photogenic pastor—neither of which I considered particularly spiritual.

Using those points for excuses, I declined the invitation.

Kelly doesn't capitulate easily, but I resisted just as staunchly. By the time we hung up the phone, she was in tears and I was miserable, knowing I'd overreacted.

How had things gotten so out of hand?

My sponsor Carol A. listened patiently as I described the situation and my remorse at the way the conversation had ended. I wanted to make an amend for hurting Kelly's feelings. But that wouldn't be a simple matter. There was no way for me to do that without reopening the subject.

Why was I so unwilling to attend a church service? Carol asked.

Well ... I just didn't *like* church.

That probably wasn't the *real* reason, she countered.

Well ... I guessed I was afraid.

Afraid of what?

Well ... maybe that I would hear or see something I wouldn't like.

Carol was unimpressed. "What would it hurt if you went

along?" she asked. "It sounds like it might be a good thing for your relationship with your daughter. And after all," she reminded me, "if you don't like it, you don't have to go back."

It was hard to argue with my sponsor's simple logic. And I couldn't attribute any evangelistic motives to her counsel. Carol was Jewish.

Humbled, I hung up the phone and called Kelly back.

* * *

Hundreds of people streamed into the church as Kelly and I found seats in the balcony. From our perch I could see potted plants arranged in an attractive backdrop around the pulpit on the stage and cast-off crutches and canes hung in prominent displays on the walls. Fortunately, I didn't have to make any negative comments about the decor. I had prayed in advance, so I was ready. I was determined to remain positive, even-tempered and non-judgmental, leaving God in charge of the evening. So I asked Kelly about her activities at the church while dozens of other conversations swirled around us.

Finally the service began with lots of singing. Then the silver-haired preacher I recognized from billboards and TV took the stage.

No wonder people came to hear him. Good looks, a powerful presentation, undeniable charisma. Plus a great message. As I listened to the sermon, long since forgotten, I wondered how the words he used, the ideas he conveyed and the Bible passages he quoted could mesh so easily with Twelve Step principles.

What a surprise.

By the time his sermon turned a corner and became an exhortation for money to support the TV ministry, I was willing to overlook the change in focus and carry away the useful parts of the experience.

That particular church collapsed in a wave of scandal a few years later. But that doesn't negate the value of my evening in its sanctuary. Tainted as the church and its pastor were by commercialism, the flaws of a messenger couldn't erase the merits of truth.

My attendance at church that night served two purposes. It established a new spiritual connection between me and my daughter. And it accentuated the requirement for open-mindedness about all things spiritual, particularly about the message of God's grace.

* * *

In Twelve Step meetings I've often heard that God is a gentleman and won't intrude where he's not welcome.

I don't agree.

While God is patient in many respects, the more I know him, the more I recognize him at work, and the more I can see that he was active in my life long before I was willing to acknowledge his presence.

I'm not sure which came first—my visit to church with Kelly or the intruder in my meditation. But God was clearly working on me.

I recently read an essay by a writer named Richard Bausch recounting an experience from his life as a Catholic schoolboy of 14. Praying one night in his room, Bausch invited God to send him a sign, some proof of his existence. "The room is quiet and quite dark," he wrote, "and abruptly I have the sense of something hovering near. There is an imminence, it seems, a deep pause in the darkness around me. I have stopped breathing. But it's more than that. Any second, it will happen—some gesture from the power and majesty. I can feel it along my spine; it is here. Here! I have never moved more swiftly in my life. I bolt out of the room as though it is on fire...."

I didn't run the morning I found the interloper in my meditation. But that finished my meditating for that morning (and for quite a time thereafter). I remember clearing away my breakfast dishes in a daze, unsettled by what I'd seen.

It wasn't the burning bush of Moses. It wasn't the blinding white light described by AA founder Bill Wilson in the *Big Book*. It wasn't the frightening "imminence" or "deep pause" of Richard Bausch.

But it was *my* spiritual experience.

It was to be quite some time before I was willing to take action on what I learned that morning. But over the months that followed I couldn't escape the reality of what had happened. Or the knowledge of who I had seen.

I couldn't escape the truth.

It was plain and simple.

At a subconscious level, even after years of evasion and denial, I was Christian.

Whether I wanted to be or not.

Boundary Lesson

When I am most profoundly challenged, I often experience the greatest leaps of growth. Sometimes God invites or urges me to reach beyond my comfort zone. But sometimes he arrives as an invader, plunging deep within, reminding me that what I foolishly imagine as my domain is, after all, his space within me.

Eyewitness Reports

"Brothers, I could not address you as spiritual but as worldly—mere infants in Christ. I gave you milk, not solid food, for you were not yet ready for it."
The Bible, I Corinthians 3:1-3

My Bible wasn't as good as Carol's.

Hers had red letters.

Other than that our Bibles were identical. The same red-tipped pages and paper-thin black leather covers: *HOLY BIBLE* (With Helps). The same dense King James language. The same murky renderings of old religious paintings: "Daniel at Prayer" by Poynter, "Jesus Purges the Temple" by El Greco. On the appropriate lines on the presentation page, my mother had printed neatly: *Connie Bovier 1947.*

I was five and Carol was eight when our parents gave us our Bibles. I treasured mine in a disconnected sort of way. I suppose I carried it with me to Sunday school during those sporadic periods when I attended. I don't recall. I do know I always granted it slightly higher status than all my other books. The Bible was definitely in a category of its own. My Bible, along with the rest of my small library, caught up with me after I left the Air Force and settled into marriage and motherhood. For years it languished untouched on a shelf, its red-edged pages fading to mottled pink, its leather binding splitting around the edges.

In 1981 when I entered my first recovery program I designated a specific bookshelf for my Twelve Step literature. Since the Twelve Steps focused on God, I finally had a logical place to shelve my aging King James Bible. For several years it stood beside my *Big Book*, *Twelve Steps and Twelve Traditions*, daily meditation books and a dozen other volumes and pamphlets about the history of the program, how to work the program and how to help others work the program.

Every year or so, as an experiment, I'd pull the Bible from the shelf, open it and scan for some point of entry into its forbidding territory. Sometimes I would read the Twenty-Third Psalm to see if my Sunday school memorization still held true. (It did.) Then I would flip through pages, sampling passages here or there, looking for something, *anything*, that offered a handhold, a connection.

I always returned the Bible to the shelf, disappointed.

I just couldn't relate.

I feared I never would.

* * *

When I'd been in recovery for seven years I reached a puzzling, dry-as-dust spiritual plateau. I was still following my prayer routine—praying morning and night and before each meal. I read program literature every day. I attended Twelve Step meetings. I sponsored women who were newer than I to recovery, encouraging their emotional and spiritual growth. I was doing everything I'd done for several years. But nothing seemed to be happening anymore in my relationship with God.

I'd grown stagnant.

An amber caution light blinked on in the back of my mind.

There's plenty of evidence to support the warning Twelve Steppers give one another about plateaus. Occasionally one needs a rest stop before a tough, new uphill climb. But more often plateaus are slippery with complacency, inducing a backward slide down spiritual hills already won.

Back into old thinking. Old behavior. Old addictions.

Although I didn't feel complacent (I wasn't even mildly content with my spiritual condition), I knew I was in a dangerous place. But more than a fear of relapse urged me forward. I *wanted* more spiritual growth. A strange new hunger gnawed at me—something I'd never experienced before.

For several years I'd been fearful of venturing outward from the safety of Twelve Step spirituality. Now I was afraid not to.

But where to from there?

* * *

One day as I considered my predicament an idea sprang to mind: why not read *A Man Called Peter*?

I knew that *A Man Called Peter* was the true story about a man of great faith. I vaguely remembered seeing the movie with my parents years before. But I had no idea why that title leaped into my consciousness at that precise moment. Maybe it was the only religious story I could think of by name. Maybe it was divine inspiration.

I considered the peculiar directive. Well, I decided, why not?

At a local bookstore I found a used paperback copy and began my friendship with Catherine Marshall. In the pages of her story I discovered that she and her late husband Peter were genuine, approachable and totally human. No insulated perfection here. They were assailed by doubts, fears and problems just as I.

To my relief I was neither spiritually singed nor deflected from any of my cherished Twelve Step principles by reading a Christian author. In fact, it not only didn't cause any harm, it felt *good*.

Soon I was back in the bookstore looking for more Catherine Marshall titles: *Beyond Our Selves*, *A Closer Walk*, *Something More*. Prowling the religion section I stumbled upon Corrie Ten Boom's inspiring autobiography, *The Hiding Place*. A Twelve Step friend recommended Og Mandino's books. Another friend recommended Hannah Hunnard's *Hinds Feet on High Places*. Someone else passed on a copy of *Guideposts* magazine.

At first I needed to excuse or overlook the religiousness of Christian writers. I skipped the parts that hinted at dogma and doctrines. Instead I listened for the authors' spirituality. In the process I began to suspect that *religious* and *spiritual* weren't mutually exclusive terms—in spite of what I'd heard from many Twelve Steppers. In spite of what I'd believed myself.

As I listened for the messages in what I read, I heard many of the same ideas upon which I'd been restructuring my life. Soon I came to accept that what these Christian writers told me about their faith was every bit as sincere and credible as the stories of faith that I heard in Twelve Step meetings.

I was growing again!

It was a heady time.

I thought more often about God. Sensing a closer connection with him than I'd felt in months, I felt a fresh new spiritual wind blowing through my life.

* * *

During my early years in recovery I'd been amply challenged by the simple faith concepts shared by other Twelve Steppers: "Act as if you believe," "Choose any Higher Power you want," "If your old God isn't working, throw him out and start over." Such ideas offered a practical place to begin and, for some time, I was so busy involving God in the daily ups and downs of my life that I had no need to reach further. I deliberately confined my spiritual reading to Twelve Step materials. I read and re-read the *Big Book* and the *Twelve and Twelve*. I studied the other books and pamphlets on my recovery bookshelf. I extracted every bit of spiritual wisdom I could find in their pages.

But just like a small child must switch from milk to solid food and learn to feed himself, eventually I needed to sink my teeth into something more demanding.

A young man in Dallas named Jim, who has founded a ministry to introduce Twelve Steppers to the God of the Bible, readily credits the Twelve Steps for saving his life. But he contends that the program can become a black hole for those who consider it a spiritual end in itself.

Even Bill Wilson, the founder of Alcoholics Anonymous, expected those who followed in his footsteps to stretch themselves further. "We are only operating a spiritual kindergarten in which people are enabled to get over drinking and find the grace to go on living to better effect," he once wrote in a letter to a friend. The *Big Book*, too, advocates exploring other resources: "Be quick to see where religious people are right. Make use of what they offer."

Thanks to some gifted Christian writers, I escaped the black hole and discovered an endless source of material to grow on.

* * *

I don't know how I knew it was time for me to read the Bible. I just knew. I also knew that my old King James version wouldn't do.

I bought a new Bible with three modern translations laid out in parallel columns with the archaic King James text. I also bought a set of Bible audiotapes. Inside the cover of my new Bible I recorded the date, December, 1989, when I began reading and listening. A year and three months later I recorded another a major milestone, the date I finished reading the Bible from beginning to end.

The *Big Book* had long been the most important volume on my bookshelves. Now the Bible (often called the *BIG, Big Book* by Christian Twelve Steppers), assumed first position, with the *Big Book* and its practical application of faith principles running a noteworthy second.

It might be argued that the dramatic conversion of St. Paul on the road to Damascus was no more profound or earthshaking than the metamorphosis of Bill Wilson from a hopeless drunk to the sober founder of a recovery movement that has transformed millions of lives. Both reports are compelling. And we have both stories on excellent authority—nothing less than the first-hand accounts of the two men themselves.

* * *

At last count I have eight or nine Bibles. They include a variety of translations and paraphrases. I have several Greek/English New Testaments that help me puzzle out the meaning of some difficult passages. Some of my Bibles have extensive study notes, some have meditative essays, some have special helps for recovering Twelve Steppers. Others are designed for travel like my 1960 pocket-sized *Scripture, Protestant, King James Version*, "presented by the United States Air Force," with my name and serial number stamped inside the cover.

I suppose I'm compulsive nowadays about Bibles. I'll use

almost any excuse to buy a new one.

Recently I did need a new one—for travel. The pockedsized New Testament that I kept in my luggage wouldn't fill the bill for my new Bible study class. Our reading assignments included the Old Testament as well.

With the approach of my birthday and an out-of-state trip, Pete and I stopped by a Christian bookstore where I found the perfect Bible for travel, a thin-line, featherweight in one of my favorite translations. Pete bought it and inscribed it with a loving message for my birthday.

On the airplane I dug my new Bible from my carry-on bag and prepared to read my class assignments. (I've come a long way from the days when I was embarrassed to pray even when home alone!) I admired the supple black leather cover, leafed through the gold-edged pages and discovered something I hadn't noticed in the store.

RED LETTERS!

Hot dog! I'm somebody now.

Reading Lesson

My spiritual development demands an open mind and open books. Whenever I need signposts for the road ahead I need only browse a bookshelf to find the encouraging stories of other spiritual pilgrims. Beginning with Twelve Step materials, moving to Christian books and ultimately to the Bible, I've found ample inspiration for my journey.

Soul Survivor

"Unless we can look the darkest, blackest fact full in the
face without damaging God's character,
we do not yet know Him."
Oswald Chambers
My Utmost for His Highest

"Good morning." My voice rings out in the apartment
complex laundry room. The small building, bright inside, is
still surrounded by darkness. But I'm wide awake. I started
my laundry earlier, before my half-hour run. Now I'm trans-
ferring an armload of wet towels from a washing machine to
a dryer before hurrying back to my apartment for a shower.

I'm on a tight schedule on Wednesday mornings. I have
an important commitment. In a short while I'm due at Bible
study.

I don't recognize the man who strides into the laundry
room. There's seldom anyone but me tackling domestic
chores so early. I expect the stranger to stop at the washers
to tend to some clothes he left there overnight.

I'm still wondering why he doesn't stop, why he doesn't respond to my greeting when he reaches me.

His right hand clamps down on my arm. Then he shows me the huge rust-tinged knife he holds in his other hand. "You come with me or I'll kill you," he says.

* * *

Easter sunrise service, 1990. Christ United Methodist Church in Farmers Branch, a suburb north of Dallas.

A cluster of folding chairs stood in the parking lot. Church members had even hauled an upright piano outdoors. In my dress and high heels I felt clueless and out of place. Only the pastor and I were dressed up. Everyone else wore jeans and sweatshirts or running outfits to ward off the chill. Listening to conversations around me, I realized that all the church regulars planned to go home after the sunrise service, returning for the more formal Easter services later that morning.

It was a stretch for me to be there at all.

I'd jogged past this particular church many times in the past. It was only a mile from the house where I'd lived during my second marriage. Now that I was single, more mindful of my need for God, now that I'd finished reading the Bible on my own, I was drawn back to this familiar building. For now I wanted help to examine and understand my Christian roots.

That's what brought me to church that Easter morning.

It was the mockingbird that encouraged me to return.

As the sunrise service began a curious mockingbird perched at the top of a small oak tree near the street, and joined in sociably as we sang a song printed in the bulletin. But that was just a warm-up. When the pastor began to speak the mockingbird cut loose with a series of riffs and trills that pealed and soared and tumbled all over themselves with such exuberance that there was no way our little cluster of worshipers could ignore it.

Giggles. Chuckles. Finally belly laughs.

I laughed at the folly of human efforts to control what goes on around us. And I laughed at the curious aptness, on resurrection morning, of people bested by a single joyful bird.

I never knew you could have so much fun in church.

* * *

The fingers are painful on my arm.

"Wait." The soles of my running shoes squeal against the linoleum floor. "Wait!"

He drags me steadily toward the door. He punctuates each plodding step with the muttered threat, "You come with me or I'll kill you."

Where is he taking me?

Outside on the darkened sidewalk we pass just feet away from a tall patio fence. Beyond the fence is the lighted kitchen window of friends.

I need to scream.

But first I need to get away from the knife.

In a second or two we'll round the corner of the building, moving away from help.

I gather my strength.

I yank as hard as I can.

The hand constricts like a vise. He swings toward me. His left arm arcs around.

Snick. Thud.

My hand flies to my face.

My fingers feel something terrible there.

* * *

"I'm interested in the Bible study you're starting this fall."

I stood anxiously in front of the minister one Sunday after worship. I'd finally worked up the courage to ask my burning question: "But I wondered ... am I too new to sign up?"

Surely there was a prerequisite, like X number of years of church attendance, or an apprenticeship period or something before a person like me could enroll in an intensive, nine-month Bible study program.

If the pastor was amused by my apprehension, he covered it well. Graciously, he assured me that I was right on time. I would fit right in. He was delighted I wanted to take part.

I could enroll! I could hardly contain myself.

My name was among the first on the list.

* * *

The flesh of my chin gapes obscenely under my fingers. The tissues swell as if my face is inflated by a pump. In the dark, liquid gushes thick and sticky over my fingers, cascading down my neck.

The feel of the rusty knife as it opened my flesh, the sound as it glanced off my jawbone, have sickened me.

Thoughts of rescue evaporate. My focus shifts to survival.

My legs blunder forward in the direction of the insistent pull. My right hand, slick with blood, fumbles at my face, trying to hold it together. Can a person bleed to death from a face wound?

The door to the fitness center, upstairs above the laundry room, is supposed to remain locked at all times. Only residents have keys.

For some reason this morning the door is unlocked. And somehow this man knows that.

* * *

The Bible study class began in September—a dozen

women led by our pastor, gathering Wednesday mornings from nine to eleven-thirty. Most of the women had religious backgrounds. Some told the group, almost sheepishly, that they'd scarcely missed a day of church in their lives. Three of us were Twelve Steppers with years of alienation from faith before we had all migrated to this church. We all listened to each other with wonder, laughing and remarking about our wildly diverse perspectives on religion, the Bible and God.

Slowly I began to learn the value of religion and the benefit of a faith community.

Along with my Twelve Steps meetings and Sunday church attendance, Wednesday morning Bible study had become a highlight of my week.

* * *

The growing light of dawn creeps through the closed mini-blinds into the fitness center. By now my friends who live across the sidewalk must be ready to leave for work. By now I should be showered and dressed, retrieving my dry laundry. Instead, downstairs, below this oddly silent room, my towels still lay in a wet tangle in a basket. My quarters for the dryer lay abandoned on the folding table.

We stand in the dim room, the two of us.

The surroundings feel strangely muffled. But what has happened stands out in sharp focus.

He grips the knife in his hand. I'm still not sure I'll survive the morning.

Physically, I have everything to lose.

Spiritually I have everything to gain.

I press my fingers against the wound in my chin. With my other hand I reach toward his arm. My fingers rest midway between his elbow and the hand that holds the knife.

He doesn't move.

His skin feels smooth and warm. I feel the pulsing of life beneath my fingers. In that surreal instant I see that he too is a beloved child of God.

With my hand on his arm, I begin to talk. I say things about God, believing every word I tell him. Then I say I need to go. I must take care of my face.

He seems surprised. He mumbles that he didn't know that he'd cut me.

My suspicion that he's on drugs increases. It's not reassuring.

"You'll call the police." He's suddenly belligerent.

I sense that he just wants to leave, to get away from what he's done. But he needs a lie he can pretend to believe.

I give him the words he must have: I just want to tend to my bleeding face.

While he thinks, I take a step or two back to give him space. To give *me* space.

At last he inches toward the stairs, still clutching the blood-drenched knife.

The seconds crawl.

"You stay right here," he growls. One last effort to remain in control. "If you come outside, I'll kill you."

He pivots. He rushes toward the stairs.

Something that's been gripping my heart drains away with every footstep that hammers down the stairs.

The door slams.

I'm shaking so hard my legs barely carry me to the window. I watch him sprint down the sidewalk toward the street.

With trembling hands I scoop together my clothes. I dress. I stumble down the stairs and out, racing in the opposite direction—toward my apartment and the telephone.

* * *

The pastor wants to visit.

"I'm fine," I say. "I'm really fine."

He says that he's sure I am, but he'd like to stop by anyway.

People want to bring food.

"Food?" I say. "I don't believe I need food ..."

They gently insist.

My ex-husband, shocked by the words of my phone call, comes by to share a meal prepared for me by my adult Sunday school class. When he sees the violent colors in my stitched and swollen face, he cries.

I nearly freeze with fear every time I open the door to leave my apartment.

A neighbor FBI agent gives me a steel baton to carry when I run. She shows me how to use it.

I work during the day in my home office.

I attend my regular Twelve Step meetings.

I do my homework for next Wednesday's Bible study.

I pray.

In church on Sunday I request prayers for my attacker.

* * *

Four months after my assault, I'm invited to tell my recovery story at a meeting not far from my home. The Friday night crowd is much larger than I expect—about two hundred people. It's Valentine's Day, a great time to talk about love. So I devote most of my talk to what I've learned about love from living and working the Twelve Step program.

I don't know until I stand at the podium whether or not I will talk about *it*. But as I look out at the faces I know someone needs to hear what I can say. So I tell what I learned about God's love one fateful day, how, in the moments my hand touched the arm of the man who assaulted me, I knew God's love radiated on him as well as on me. I tell how it was the assurance of God's unwavering love that sustained me through the experience.

The phone call comes early the next morning.

A friend, voice intense, asks if I will call a woman who heard me speak the night before. She has only a year or so of Twelve Step recovery, he says, and she desperately needs to talk. After the meeting, she spent several hours with friends, then went home to her house where she was beaten and raped by an intruder. During her attack she clung to the knowledge that I'd survived my assault physically, emotionally and spiritually. She kept telling herself throughout her ordeal that if I could survive *so could she*.

She and I talk many times during the following weeks and months. We talk about survival and about strength. We talk about the untouchable core that no one and no act of violence can ever touch. We talk about free will and judgment and retribution and forgiveness.

We talk about God.

Together we read from the *Twelve and Twelve*: "Can we transform (our) calamities into assets, sources of growth and comfort to ourselves and those about us? Well, we surely have a chance ... if we are willing to receive that grace of God which can sustain and strengthen us in any catastrophe."

* * *

Snick. Thud.

I won't forget the feeling, the sound.

Snick. Thud.

So much blood from a little wound.

I think about other wounds—far deeper than mine— wounds made with the ring of hammer against nails, resounding around the world and down through the centuries.

So much blood.

Enough to wash away every sin.

Even his?
Yes. Even his.

Free Will Lesson

Learning about God includes accepting the terrible implications of free will. It can be tragic and painful to be part of another's spiritual tests, as the sick and suffering face opportunities to break down the barriers that isolate them from God. And I believe God sorrows over the evil choices of estranged souls as much as he rejoices over the right choices of those who strive for obedience.

No one said this lesson would be easy.

Missing Ingredient

"My attitude toward prayer has changed drastically over the years .... as I look back, I realize those early attempts were mostly begging sessions....That's not where I am now. Asking is still a big part of prayer, but I've also learned other aspects, such as fellowship and praise."
Cecil Murphey
Invading the Privacy of God

In 1993 Pete and I packed all my belongings into a rental truck in Dallas and headed south on Interstate 45 toward Houston, arriving in the early evening at his townhome south of the city in Seabrook.

My new home.

Our home.

For months after the move, I existed in a semi-dazed state. It was almost more than I could believe—the circumstances, the divine benevolence if you will, that had placed this exceptional man in my life.

When I'd met Pete the last thing I expected was to fall in

love again. In my early fifties by then, I'd already had a thirteen-year first marriage, a ten-year second marriage and between them I'd loved a man who died. Although each heart alliance had ended painfully, I'd grown through each relationship and I had no regrets. In fact, I felt blessed by more than my share of love.

So I was hardly expecting Pete.

I was working the day I met him, researching an article for an aviation magazine, observing a training class for pilots from the rear of a chilly classroom. Pete was one of two pilots team-teaching the course.

As I took notes about the course content, I was soon distracted from my task by watching Pete. His interaction with class members revealed an easy self-confidence, a comfort level with emotions and a genuine interest in people that I would have valued enormously in a friend.

Hmmm, I thought. *Interesting. This is probably the kind of guy I should have been looking for all of my life.*

That evening when I told my daughter about my new acquaintance, I still considered it a chance meeting in the workplace. Even when I arranged to interview Pete some few months later for another article, I never dreamed that within a year I'd be moving to Houston so we could share our lives.

.* * *

I suppose I was too much in love to notice the stifling heat and humidity during my first September in Houston, but the weather seemed glorious. Pete's flying schedule took him away for several days every week, so I had plenty of time to myself to write and to think—which suited my personality and my work habits just fine. As usual, God seemed to know just what he was doing when he matched the two of us.

Many mornings my exercise routine took me to a beautiful park near our home where a path wound through the rolling landscape, skirting a playground, picnic tables and barbecue grills. Veering from the path I often detoured onto a fishing pier jutting out over the water. There on the pier one morning, as water lapped at the pilings below and seagulls cried overhead, I felt so bathed in blessings—unwarranted, unexpected, undeserved, unearned—that simple gratitude just wasn't enough.

Heart filled to bursting, I had no sufficient means for expressing my joy.

* * *

Many people, especially frustrated relatives, wonder why men and woman in recovery who attend church still feel compelled to go to Twelve Step meetings.

Why should anyone need both?

The primary reason first: Twelve Steppers often continue to attend meetings even after turning to organized religion because there's enormous potential for losing focus on the seriousness of an addiction when not exposed regularly to others who share the problem. Denial *always* lies in wait. Family and friends who don't understand addictions can be downright dangerous if they try to shame or embarrass an addict for dependence on the program. "You haven't had a problem for a month (a year, ten years, twenty years) now. How come you still want to go to *those meetings?*"

Yet those who've been around Twelve Step programs for any length of time can cite numerous examples of men and women who've returned to addictions when relying on church alone to maintain their recovery and their relationship with God.

That's the main reason for continuing to attend Twelve Step meetings.

Personally I have a second reason, one that's particularly meaningful for me: *the Twelve Step program makes far greater demands upon me for emotional maturity than does the church.*

It's been my experience that the church overlooks a host of problematic character traits in members simply because they're below the blatant threshold of "sins" and because fine-tuning annoying personalities is beyond the church's purview.

By contrast the Twelve Steps are all about personal change. The steps provide concrete instructions that not only nurture spirituality but enlist God's help to improve relationships, to handle negative emotions and to deal with a whole range of other behavioral issues. Sponsors and friends in recovery often confront those who persist in bad attitudes and questionable actions. And meetings offer powerful reminders of the need for continual change as life circumstances evolve.

Well then, if the Twelve Step program provides so many benefits, why do I need church?

For me there's a reason as convincing and powerful as the reasons I keep close to the program. *The church expects far more of me spiritually than do the Twelve Step fellowships.*

When I was new in recovery in the early '80s the liberal, choose-your-own spirituality of the Twelve Steps suited me just fine. But once I began to know God, once I began attending church, I found myself adopting, and wanting, increasingly higher standards.

These new standards included less attention to how much love I *receive*, and more emphasis on how much love I *give*.

To family. To friends. To others in the world.

And to God.

* * *

I suppose I gravitate toward acronyms because I have a disorderly mind. As an antidote to lazy brain, I've installed an extensive array of mental collection bins for organizing new information. I like practical labels—the Twelve Steps were ready made for my way of thinking—and acronyms are perfect for the job.

I first heard about ACTS when the minister of my church in Dallas mentioned it during a Bible study class. ACTS sounded like a nice, handy formula for prayer.

Adoration.

Confession.

Thanksgiving.

Supplication.

Thanksgiving and supplication were long-time friends. I'd long exercised "please" and "thank you" prayers as the bookends that framed my day. And prayers of confession were almost as familiar because I'd shared my shortcomings and my inventories with God and a sponsor on more than one occasion.

Since I was already using most of the ACTS checklist, I doubted that I needed its help. Nevertheless, I tucked it away in memory, just in case.

So when I'd moved to Houston, when I'd paused on the lakeside pier to contemplate my new life, when I couldn't think of any other way to express adequate appreciation, I remembered ACTS. Reciting the four words to myself, I realized that my life had totally ignored the first kind of prayer—the prayer of adoration.

At first I felt silly even *thinking* about adoration. Babies, kittens and puppies were adorable. But, God? In the dictionary I discovered that the primary meaning of *adore* encompasses honor, reverence, respect, esteem—terms all perfectly apropos of a supreme being.

Adore also meant loving God—not for any ulterior or self-centered motive, but simply because he was my creator.

In church I began to pay closer attention to the words and actions of the worship service. And I began to see the opportunities to love God, to *adore* him, through public as well as private prayer.

* * *

A friend phoned one Saturday afternoon to say she'd just written a brief Fourth Step inventory and needed to share it with someone. Her sponsor was out of town. Would I hear it? Of course I would.

After she read what she'd written, we discussed it briefly. Then she heaved a big sigh of relief. "Thanks," she said. "Now I can go to confession."

She, a devout Catholic, and I, an equally committed Protestant, had arrived at the same conclusion about the most effective approach to recovery.

We do our Twelve Step work first. We do church second. But we do them both.

In the Twelve Steps I gained the priceless knowledge that God loves me.

In church I've gained an equally precious enlightenment— that it's my privilege, my opportunity and my obligation to love him back.

Finally I understood what had drawn me to church.

Worship Lesson

I once basked in the love of my "newly discovered" God. But mature love is a two-way relationship and much is required of me as well. Today I walk a far more demanding path, knowing that what I need for further development isn't more petitions for my wants and imagined needs, but placing myself before God with no motive other than to love him.

Global Positioning

"The loftiest and surest way to heaven is measured
by desires and not by miles."
Anonymous
The Cloud of Unknowing

I'm a cheap date when it comes to travel. I don't like expensive restaurants. I'm not much of a shopper. I don't crave costly entertainments. Just stick me in the passenger seat, hand me a map and I'm happy.

The map is the crucial part.

I like maps. I *need* maps. For me, maps are serious business.

When I travel by air I appreciate the route maps in seatback pockets, and I like thoughtful cockpit crews who provide useful commentary about landmarks below.

Traveling by car I keep a roadmap on my lap or right beside me so I can grab it at a moment's notice. My husband is often content to trust highway signage for brief trips, but I prefer to keep track of where we are and what's coming up.

I like to monitor our progress, ticking off towns and exits as we move from city to city, crease to crease, across the printed landscape.

My preoccupation with maps has become a running joke. "Likely story," Pete teases me when I suggest a stop for coffee or a restroom break. "You just want to buy another map." I admit it.

I always want to know where I am.

Without tangible reference points I feel unsettled, precarious—like an untethered kite or a runaway balloon.

* * *

When I was ten years old I lived in Eugene, Oregon, and there I fell headlong into first love with the boy next door. The studious son of a school principal, Stephen introduced me to stamp collecting and, because he took the hobby seriously, so did I. Although my family moved away after a couple of years, postage stamps continued to fascinate me. I learned about geography from stamps. And that's how I learned about the natural and political boundaries of our world.

Somewhere in the process, I grew intensely interested in where I fit in.

I can relate to the current generation of road warriors, pilots and mariners enraptured by the Global Positioning System. Imagine using satellite signals to pinpoint one's precise location while motoring about on, or relatively near, the face of the earth. If I weren't so resistant to technology, I'd probably own a GPS receiver of my own.

It once seemed that I had a simple fixation on knowing my physical location. But I've concluded there's more to it than that.

Whenever I attend a business meeting, a class or a seminar, I'm never completely at ease until I have an agenda or outline in my hand.

When I upgraded my computer, I obsessively filled a shelf with books about my new system and software, placing a fat manual for Word 97 between my monitor and CPU.

When I attend a ballet or a musical, I always choose seats in the balcony. The price is great. The view is even better. From the balcony I can see the pattern of the choreography. With my little binoculars I can zoom in on costumes, scenery and individual performers. But from the balcony, with the naked eye *and with program notes in hand*, I can see everything, understand everything and follow the grand sweep of the story.

From the balcony I enjoy a godlike view.

Once on a business trip I stayed in a hotel where the lobby was lined with mirrors. Everywhere I looked were mirrored walls, pillars, doors. Was I looking at real or reflected people? Were those the real doorways? Where was the real main desk? Where were the real elevators? I felt as if I'd stepped into a nightmarish episode of the *Twilight Zone.*

Disoriented, unable to separate reality from reflection, I remained off balance (and resentful at the architect) until it was time to pack up and escape that disturbing hotel.

* * *

A few years ago I attended a Catholic funeral where I sat with a friend, a Protestant like me, who appointed herself keeper of the bulletin. The problem was that she kept tucking the bulletin in the pew rack ahead of her or laying it down on the seat beside her. As the priest moved through the liturgy my friend repeatedly had to retrieve our bulletin and locate the right place. We remained several beats behind throughout the entire service. By the time we'd missed the beginning of several responsive readings and fumbled through the hymnal during the first verse of several songs, I wanted to yell "Enough already!" and yank the bulletin from her hand.

God gives me great opportunities for personal insights when I find myself angry in church.

I could almost hear my late sponsor Carol A. muttering, "There you go again, Connie, trying to control everything. You can't bear for someone else to be in charge of instructions that you think affect you. Why can't you relax and let God be in charge?"

I've been confounded over the years by the dogged persistence of my ego in its attempts to re-exert control. I've turned my life over to God thousands of times, only to discover new subtle ways my *self* tries to snatch certainty and security in the midst of an unstable, constantly changing world.

I can see that much of my life had been guided by three questions:

Where am I?

Where am I going?

And what comes next along the way?

* * *

The notice about centering prayer appeared in our church newsletter.

I had no idea what to expect when I signed up for the class. I just knew that I wanted to learn more about prayer so the class was sure to be interesting. From the first meeting I knew that centering prayer, a prayer of silence that some call Christian meditation, was ideal for Twelve Steppers.

The guidelines were simple: Sit relaxed, upright, with eyes closed and feet on floor. I was to choose a sacred word, a symbol of my intention to be present to God's presence and action within me. Whenever I became aware of thoughts I was to release them gently and use my sacred word to return to God. Simple enough.

Between classes I tried centering prayer at home, but only

a time or two. In spite of its intellectual appeal, I didn't feel called to continue. Somehow the time wasn't right. So I forgot about centering prayer for more than a year.

Then I reached a new place in my spiritual growth and began feeling a call to move more closely toward God. Without fuss or resistance, I began the discipline of twenty minutes of centering every morning after I awoke.

In spite of my use of a sacred word, my mind kept reaching for an image, some location, some sense of place or time to anchor my prayer experience.

Where was I supposed to be looking for God?

Where's the path? I wondered.

Up? Down? Within?

Are we there yet?

Where are the rest of the directions?

* * *

About this time I attended a Twelve Step meeting where several experienced sailors told of hair-raising experiences at sea. I've always felt that drowning must be a horrible kind of death, so I squirmed through their graphic stories, even though they were using their tales to illustrate an increase in faith. I left that meeting knowing far more than I'd ever wanted to know about the hazards of sailing. I also left uncomfortably aware that my fear of drowning was related directly to a lack of reliance upon God.

Searching one day for more resources about centering prayer, I happened upon a fourteenth century spiritual classic, *The Cloud of Unknowing*. The anonymous author warns beginners against taking too literally the directional words used by their spiritual advisors. "I insist that our contemplative work shall not be directed up or down, to this side or that, forward or backward, as if it were a machine," he wrote. "For it is not a work of the flesh but an interior vital adventure pursued in the spirit."

An interior adventure. Pursued not in the mind. Not in the flesh. But in the spirit.

What if I were to pretend, in spirit, that my movement into prayer was my resignation to *drowning in God?*

Ahhhgh.

I was still struggling with this unappealing idea when I saw the science fiction adventure movie *Alien 3.* The ending stunned me. After the hero Ripley (Sigourney Weaver) destroys the last adult alien, she knows that she too must die or she'll place the human race in peril once again with the infant alien that's incubating within her.

Ripley positions herself on a catwalk high in an off-world leadworks and pauses with her back to the roiling cauldron below. She leans out, extending her arms, and her slender body forms a cross as she falls in breath-stopping slow motion, down, down, toward the molten lead.

Absolute abandonment.

Do I have one half, one quarter the courage of a fictional movie hero?

Can I surrender my questions: Where am I? Where am I going? What comes next?

Can I relinquish my maps, my self-determined destinations, my powerful need to know?

Am I willing to stand on a precipice, to fall without reference points into the uncharted, indefinable space that is God?

Am I willing to drown in him?

Geography Lesson

I must surrender my insistence upon knowing where I am physically, emotionally or spiritually. I must be willing to fling myself into the unknown without demands or expectations, without previews or guarantees, trusting in the process for the strengthening of my faith.

Cloud of Witnesses

"Therefore, since we are surrounded by such a great cloud
of witnesses, let us throw off everything that hinders
and ... let us run with perseverance the race
marked out for us."
The Bible; Hebrews 12:1

"Have you considered getting a spiritual director?"

I was startled by John's question. In my reading I'd seen
references to spiritual direction, but I'd assumed it was
something meant for people much further along in personal development than I. I'd never thought of it as something for me. John went on to say that two of his clergy
friends counseled regularly with spiritual directors and if I
ever wanted to pursue the subject he'd be happy to get me
some referrals.

Pete and I had met John and Nita for dinner in an Italian
restaurant. Nita was the associate pastor of our church, her
husband John, the pastor of another local church. It seemed
we were destined to be friends. By unspoken agreement we

skimmed over the typical get-acquainted small talk and, by the time we finished our salad and breadsticks, we were comfortably discussing our marriages, our personal histories and our careers.

I had just given a thumbnail description of my Twelve Step recovery and my subsequent return to church, when I added that I'd been in a state of spiritual confusion for some months. Lately I'd experienced the strange sensation that God was *pulling* me—not guiding or pushing or beckoning, but drawing me forward.

That's when John asked his question.

As we moved on to other topics, part of my mind lingered on his words. The mention of spiritual direction had landed squarely in the center of a dilemma that I hadn't, until now, put into words.

Where to from here?

* * *

Where had all these ministers come from anyway?

Suddenly it seemed as if I were surrounded.

Unlike my husband, who'd been an altar boy and assisted priests in worship, I'd had no contact at all with ordained clergy before my forties. The closest I'd come to knowing a pastor personally was the Baptist preacher cousin of a former in-law who made an annual appearance at a family gathering on Christmas Eve. He read the Christmas story from the Bible and said a prayer—a mildly embarrassing religious blip in the evening—before he left for other commitments and our Christmas celebration settled into a familiar, secular Santa Claus mode.

To my old way of thinking ministers occupied pedestals. Remote, vaguely mysterious, they possessed a superior connection with God that no one else could attain.

Ministers weren't like other people.

They certainly weren't like me.

At my first church I was shocked to hear the familiar way members of the congregation addressed the pastor. Good heavens! You mean you could call a minister by his first name? My brain seized up just thinking of it. Addressing him as reverend in the informal atmosphere of our church seemed hopelessly stuffy, but even when I could say his first name, it never rolled off my tongue with ease.

A few years after moving to Houston I felt more comfortable around pastors. By then I'd come to know the clergy at our church through involvement on committees. Pete and I were good friends with a retired minister and his wife in our congregation. And my weekly Tuesday morning breakfast gathering included a clergy woman from another denomination.

What a curious turn of events.

I was surrounded by a cloud of witnesses.

What did God have in mind?

* * *

In the months following our first dinner with John and Nita, I had several occasions to travel on business. It seemed I couldn't get on an airplane without meeting another minister.

I spent one flight visiting with a congenial Southern Baptist who was on his way home from a clergy training event. On another flight I found myself in a middle seat between a woman minister from a non-denominational church in the Midwest and a young daughter of missionaries who was writing her dissertation on Biblical references in the Victorian novel to earn her English Ph.D.

Fascinated by such "chance" meetings and by our clergy friends I noticed a distinct shift in my attitude. I still believed that ministers were answering a lofty call but the down-to-earth demeanor of those I knew intrigued me.

They didn't expect me to stand in awe of them or their profession.

They seemed more like me, more *human*, than I would ever have guessed.

Most important, these clergy connections snuffed out any lingering arrogance I may have had about the superiority of Twelve Step spirituality. My minister friends were living their religious beliefs with the same diligence and devotion as my role models of spiritual rigor in Twelve Step recovery. What's more, these ministers' assurance of God's reality and his presence through every one of life's trials bore witness to rich, resilient faith that I hoped I too might someday attain.

And sometimes they functioned as holy messengers, providing pieces of my own spiritual puzzle.

* * *

During an extended layover in the Phoenix airport one evening my laptop computer attracted the attention of another woman awaiting a flight to Houston. She asked about my work and reciprocated by telling me she was involved in theatre. We had a brief interchange about writing and drama before she moved away.

By the time our flight boarded I happily anticipated a couple of hours immersed in a new mystery novel I'd bought in the airport bookstore. As I walked down the aisle of the nearly empty aircraft, the woman from the gate lounge invited me to take the seat beside her. I hesitated, wanting to plead work or reading. But an inner nudge told me this was not the time to indulge my introverted self.

So I accepted her invitation and sat down.

Settling in for the flight we picked up the thread of our earlier conversation and I asked her to tell me more about her work. She explained that the theater she directed was affiliated with a church. Oh? She was a Presbyterian minister, in fact, assigned with her minister husband to pastor a large congregation in a small southern California town.

I should have known.

This woman was such a pleasant companion that the flight passed quickly as we discussed her call to ministry, her experience in seminary during the 70's and how she and her husband managed their entwined careers. Describing her husband's job as senior pastor of their church, she added that he had many compelling interests. "Just recently," she said, "he was certified as a spiritual director."

The statement struck with electric force.

By the time the lights of Houston appeared and the 737 banked southward, lining up for approach to Hobby Airport, I'd learned all my seatmate could tell me about spiritual direction.

I had only one question left: "How does someone know when the time is right?"

She asked what I was feeling.

I described the persistent tugging, the *pull*.

She listened for a few seconds. "You sound ripe," she said.

She went on to say that she wasn't familiar with the religious community in Houston. But she felt certain I could find someone who could point me toward resources.

I just happened to know someone who could.

Mentor Lesson

God sometimes calls me to growth by placing unexpected guides along my path, especially at junctures when I most need more information, new suggestions, renewed vision or deeper assurance for my journey.

Hitting the Wall

"If you write for God you will reach many men and bring them joy. If you write for men—you may make some money and you may give someone a little joy and you may make a noise in the world, for a little while. If you write only for yourself you can read what you yourself have written and after ten minutes you will be so disgusted you will wish that you were dead."
Thomas Merton
New Seeds of Contemplation

Sorting through the mail at my desk, I spotted the magazine and quickly flipped through the first few pages. There. My book review.

I had to smile at the irony.

There was my name all right. But I was the reviewer, not the author.

The book was *Red Line*, a mystery novel featuring an Alaskan bush pilot, written by Megan Mallory Rust. It was the second of Megan's books that I'd reviewed for *Aviation for Women*, a publication for which I also wrote feature articles.

I read the review and closed the magazine with a sigh. I enjoyed supporting the success of another writer, but I couldn't help glancing at the side of my desk, at my own aviation mystery, still in manuscript form, housed in a three-ring notebook.

Lately I'd felt like a character in a slapstick cartoon, picking myself up, brushing myself off, shaking my head in befuddlement. I'd just spent the last year and a half charging full speed straight into a wall.

* * *

I could have sworn the idea came straight from God.

The concept for a series of mystery novels sprang full blown into my mind one day about an hour north of Houston on Interstate 45. I was on my way to Dallas to attend the monthly meeting of my writers group and the funeral of one of our long-time members. Only a year earlier, before the onset of cancer, Marianne Verges had published *On Silver Wings*, an inspiring history about the WASPS of World War II. Marianne and I were among the few non-fiction writers in our group and, because we shared a specialty in aviation, we'd enjoyed a unique bond. During the last months of her life we'd even discussed a possible collaboration on her second book, a biography of an early woman aviator.

As I drove my reflections on Marianne's abruptly curtailed career led to thoughts about my own work, in particular, my fiction. I mulled over some germinating ideas and two characters returned to mind—a woman and a man I'd long envisioned as the central figures in a short story.

That's when it happened—the idea.

This couple didn't belong in a short story. Nothing so limited as that. They belonged in a mystery novel …. no, in a *series* of mystery novels ... set in the aviation industry. She, the amateur sleuth. He, a friend and love interest. It was perfect! Why hadn't I thought of this before?

After all, my goal, *my expectation*, was to become a novelist. After years of writing advertising and business materials, I'd finally completed one novel and written the first draft of a second. But those efforts fell into the hard-to-sell *literary* category and even an agent who believed in my work was unable to find a publisher for my first, completed book.

But here was a concept that could work.

With millions of devoted fans, mysteries had a much better chance for publication than literary novels. What's more, a series of books set in the aviation industry would allow me to integrate the fiction and non-fiction aspects of my work. At last I'd have an outlet for all the extra research and for all the personal views that had no place in factual magazine articles.

Besides, no writer was producing books along the lines I had in mind. Authors like Megan Rust could craft exciting stories from a pilot's viewpoint. But I, a non-pilot, could offer an observer's perspective on broader areas that interested me—like pilot training and career development, human factors and aviation safety.

I could create my own sub-niche in the mystery field.

With one hand I fumbled a notebook from my briefcase and propped it on the steering wheel to jot down the premises for one, two, three, *four* books in the series.

This was phenomenal. I'd never had such a sweeping concept for my work.

Best of all the idea appeared flawless.

Still, a little caution flag began waving in the back of my mind.

I'd loved reading mysteries for years, but I'd never tried writing one. My character-driven short stories and unpublished novels were a far cry from plot-driven commercial fiction. Could I learn everything I would need to know?

Could I develop a convincing story line around the core idea for the first book? Was I really prepared to tackle another book-length project with no assurance of success? I refused to be intimidated by the risks or by the steep learning curve I saw ahead. After all, I believed the idea was inspired. I was convinced that God had offered it so I would reach and grow, so I would claim some new territory in my craft.

By the time I reached Dallas, I knew that a mystery novel would be my next project. Attending Marianne's funeral, I could almost hear her cheering me on.

* * *

My friend Gisela is an expert at tough love. From the time we met in the mid-1980s she's given me little latitude for whining about my work. Back in those days I was challenged continually by the feast-or-famine nature of free lance writing.

"Do you realize what you're doing?" she asked me one day. "You're either complaining that you don't have enough work and you don't know how you'll pay your bills, or you're complaining that you're swamped with projects and don't know how you'll meet all your deadlines."

I wasn't thrilled by her insight. I'd been living the Twelve Steps long enough to know that fretting was good evidence that, once again, I was forgetting to rely on God. Eventually I learned to appreciate Gisela's honesty and began working the steps more diligently in relation to my work.

When I moved from Dallas in 1993, I left virtually all of my advertising clients behind and my career entered a new phase. Now my time was divided between magazine articles and fiction. My conversations with Gisela changed as well.

During our visits we talked more about my drive to express myself in novels and short stories. Once as I bemoaned the fact that I *had* to write, she scolded me gently. "You don't *have* to write, Connie. No one is forcing you. You *get* to write."

Self-absorbed with my career struggles, I'd never seriously considered my writing a gift from God to me. When I focused on the difficulties of producing and marketing my words, it was easier to view writing as a punishment than a privilege.

My friend also possessed an uncanny ability to detect ego entanglements in my work. Whenever I bewailed rejections on my stories or my first novel, she'd contend that it was my pride that told me I must be published.

It was easy for me to brush off such comments. After all, Gisela wasn't a writer. She couldn't possibly understand the hunger of a writer to see her work in print.

Only novices and wannabes write for themselves, I would counter. Writers who don't submit their work for publication are either unwilling to apply the time and energy it takes to learn the craft and develop marketing skills, or fear the rejections that submission almost always entails.

"Professional writers write for publication," I insisted.

* * *

Returning home to Houston from the writers meeting and Marianne's funeral I stormed my local used bookstore. I bought and read mysteries by the dozen, examining how various authors handled series characters and plots. I read every book available about mystery fiction. I flew to conferences dedicated to mystery writers, editors and fans. I registered for classes about the mystery genre. I joined Mystery Writers of America and Sisters in Crime, devouring their newsletters and haunting the events they sponsored.

Meanwhile, I planned and plotted my own book.

By the time I sat at the keyboard and typed chapter one, I

knew where my story was going, how it would get there and how the mystery would be resolved.

I also knew that this novel, unlike my first one, *would be published*. And I told everyone so. "I'm determined to write a successful book," I said to my husband, my family, my friends, other writers, "no matter how long or how many drafts it takes."

A year and a half later I read the first chapter to my writers critique group in Dallas.

Their response was disheartening. Not quite, they said. It's just not there yet.

I rewrote chapter one to create a stronger lead and read it again to my writer friends.

Huh-uh, they said. Not yet.

At the same time responses were trickling in from my first round of readers in Houston—politely encouraging remarks about the characters and the story. The lack of enthusiasm was thunderous. Worse yet, the agent who'd tried to sell my first book rejected the mystery outright.

Finally I asked one trusted writer friend to read the entire manuscript and give me a no-holds-barred critique. She did. While the story had many good points, she said, it lacked sufficient tension. It wasn't a page-turner. And a commercial novel, certainly a commercial mystery novel, *must* be a page-turner.

I thanked her and took several paces backward.

I'd been writing long enough to know that four drafts were barely a start for many ultimately successful novels. Hadn't I spent seven years writing and rewriting my first book? Hadn't I just heard one novelist describe the grueling fourteen rewrites it took to get her first mystery published?

But how could I be so far off the mark after so much preparation? What had gone wrong?

Had I fallen into one of my own traps? Did I think that just because I was pursuing a God-given idea, that just because

I'd taken all the steps I felt would ensure success, I automatically would produce a marketable novel? In building up my expectations had I set myself up instead for failure?

Bandaging my wounded pride, I slipped into a period of confusion, totally unable to regenerate the enthusiasm I'd once felt for the book. Without a sense of direction, how could I bring myself to begin the deep revisions the novel required?

As I worked on other writing projects, my mind reeled with questions.

Had I hit a blank wall? Maybe I just wasn't meant to write a commercial mystery novel.

Had I missed the door? Maybe I just needed to rethink my plot and my characters and begin revisions regardless of how I felt.

Had I collided with a door labeled NOT YET? Maybe, as much as I cared about my characters and story, the mystery was merely another practice novel, not the book that would carry me into the now-published realm.

* * *

As often happens when I'm mired down in my life, God began to work on me through others.

One day as I described to Gisela my quandary about the mystery novel, I couldn't resist trying again to explain why publication was so important to me.

"Writing is communicating," I said, "and a writer is completed by the reader. But without publication that can't happen. *Reaching the reader is what writing is all about.*" I sat back, certain that I'd finally expressed myself in a way she would understand.

"Why don't you stop worrying about reaching the reader?" she asked. "Think instead about reaching God."

I was speechless.

For years I'd imagined myself doing God's work by serving others through my work. In my business writing and non-fiction I always provided useful and accurate information for readers. In my fiction I aimed directly for the heart, hoping to help others feel a little less isolated.

Nothing wrong with those intentions—except perhaps that they were self determined. Just as I'd decided years before that becoming a published novelist was necessary for my success in life, perhaps I'd been determining how I would relate to God in my work.

But what did I know about *reaching* him?

* * *

Another day. Another conversation. Another friend, this one a published writer. In the hotel room we shared at a writers conference, as we sat on our beds talking, I confessed my childhood goal of writing successful novels and my puzzlement about the mystery. After all, I said, that was to have been my route to success.

But where was success?

What was success?

How was I ever going to discern what God wanted me to do?

I was even more perplexed, I told her, because God had been prodding me to begin a totally different book, one that wasn't even fiction, a *spiritual book* for heaven's sake. Wouldn't it be easier for all concerned if he'd just show me how to re-work the mystery?

She smiled. "Why don't you try surrendering all your writing dreams to God," she suggested softly. "Why not let him take all of them. Then wait to see what part he gives back to you."

She smiled again. She knew how much she was asking.

Career Lesson

If I am to live a seamless life of faith, God consciousness must infuse every aspect of my career. I must challenge myself not only to celebrate spiritual values in and through my work but to trust that God will define my success, not necessarily in the ways I would have it appear, but in ways that he knows are right for me.

Resounding Symbols

All manner of thing shall be well
When the tongues of flame are in-folded
Into the crowned knot of fire
And the fire and the rose are one.
T.S. Eliot
"Four Quartets, Little Gidding"

When I lived in north Dallas my morning run often followed a jogging trail that wound around the campus perimeter of Brookhaven College. In dry weather, I scarcely noticed the number of ant hills that bordered the asphalt path. But after one Texas-sized downpour, dozens of mounds erupted overnight—great masses of damp soil dredged from flooded underground chambers, heaped up on the surface like fluffy brown melons.

It was an incredible sight.

I began to make a point of running the campus route after heavy rains. How did the ants survive these onslaughts? What instinct triggered such arduous excavations of their flooded nests? But I wasn't after the scientific facts that govern ant colonies. I was after something deeper. My mind simply couldn't shake off the image of those post-disaster recoveries. It was many months before I grasped the meaning of the ants.

* * *

I love talking to other writers about writing. At conferences I enjoy leading workshops that help introduce beginners to various aspects of the craft. A couple of years ago I chose for my topic the use of symbolism in short stories.

When I started preparing for the workshop I didn't have a clue what I would say—just some vague notion about the relationship between symbol and theme. It had been years since I'd taken an English course that addressed the function of theme in fiction. And in my own work I'd been so busy trying to master the elements of character and plot that I hadn't given much thought to the underlying message. Yet a literary agent had pointed out to me that many of my short stories incorporated symbols, one reason why those particular stories were successful.

Since I'd never analyzed the thematic content of my fiction, developing this workshop gave me the perfect opportunity to satisfy my curiosity. What did symbols have to do with the deeper meanings in my work? Was it the presence of a symbol that caused the theme of a story to materialize, seemingly by itself?

Reading some of my published work with these questions in mind, I saw the connections. In one story, a pair of sturdy work gloves left behind in the fork of a tree embody a dying woman's hope for escaping her cancer-riddled body. In another, finding a child's lost toy mirrors a couple's rediscovery of the love they thought they'd lost. In a third story,

I spotted the resilient ants from Brookhaven College. They'd resurfaced in a suburban back yard, symbolizing the efforts of a woman and her husband to dig themselves out from the emotional devastation of a crushing family secret. Examining these stories and the stories of other writers, I saw that symbols weren't merely literary devices, a technique to make comprehension tough for the reader. Actually they carry much of a story's dramatic energy. When used effectively, they can make a story more resonant, more real. Within a symbol, the true significance of a story often resides.

What makes symbols so powerful? There's a simple answer.

Symbols bypass the intelligence, evading the mind's insistence upon logic and clarity and definition. Symbols speak directly to the heart.

And symbols are the means by which God often communicates with me.

* * *

For several years I worked at an advertising agency in Dallas where employees decorated their cubicles with wild and wacky abandon. My ever-expanding collage of cat pictures, cartoons and memorabilia was pretty tame compared to some of the décor. But amidst all the feline trappings in my work space hung one odd, unrelated piece, a large matted photograph that I never quite understood.

I'm not sure how the photo migrated to my office in the first place. I probably found it in a storeroom, abandoned by someone who'd moved on to a new job. But a part of me had recognized something in the photo and claimed it as mine.

The focal point of the picture was a tall, metal gate, a garden gate, surrounded by a tangle of vegetation. The gate itself wasn't forbidding. But the photo had an unsettling effect. The scene on one side of the gate lay in shadow. Beyond the gate spread a sunny landscape.

The intriguing aspect of the picture was its perspective. The viewer stood within the enclosure in a shady thicket, while just ahead stood the gate ... wide open.

I didn't particularly enjoy the picture. Yet it followed me through several restructurings of our modular offices, always reappearing on my wall. But after several years at the advertising agency, when I resigned to begin my own free lance business, I packed up all my cat clutter but left the picture behind.

I suppose I no longer needed it. I'd received its message at an unconscious level.

By then I was in Twelve Step recovery.

Finally (perhaps like the picture's previous owner) I'd stepped out of my self-imposed prison, leaving a troubled and shadowy part of my life behind.

* * *

Growing up in the Pacific Northwest I'm on intimate terms with rainbows. They're one benefit of the rainy climate and almost (but not quite) compensate for an appalling population of moisture-loving slugs. Once when I hadn't visited Seattle for many years, as I drove from Sea-Tac Airport across a valley and up a hill toward my cousin's home in Renton, a magnificent double rainbow greeted me. I happily counted it a personal *welcome home.*

In Washington rainbows are practically part of the landscape. That's not so in Texas. Here rainbows are comparatively rare. And when I do see one, I'm usually disappointed by its tentative pastels and fleeting presence.

I've been guilty of smugness about this. Being a web-footed Washingtonian, I know a *real* rainbow when I see one.

About a year ago God put me in my place.

I'd been mildly disgruntled for some time with the

progress of my career and on one particularly ungrateful day I abandoned my computer to take care of household errands. Right in synch with my mood, a growling thunderstorm churned in from the Gulf of Mexico, dumped its load of rain on the afternoon traffic and rumbled off to the north. As I climbed from my dripping car at the post office, I noticed people standing around their cars, pointing, talking to each another. I looked up and there across the eastern sky spread a rainbow more brilliant than anything I'd ever seen, its colors so vivid and distinct that the arch appeared painted on the backdrop of dark clouds and patchy blue.

After several admiring minutes, I hurried inside to retrieve my mail. Then I drove away slowly, still sneaking incredulous peeks at the sky. Near home I couldn't resist the child's game of searching for the rainbow's end. Maybe a rainbow this dazzling would have more substance than those half-hearted wisps of color that faded into inconsequence high above the ground.

Rounding a curve in the road, I laughed aloud. The north end of the rainbow, still vivid, dropped straight into a cluster of homes. Quickly I scanned for the opposite end of the arch. And there it was, plunging into the water of Clear Lake just beyond my own backyard. The full spectrum of colors shimmered on the rippling surface, a halo of radiance around the point of contact.

At home I returned to my computer, smiling.

The day had turned to shining gold.

* * *

Pete and I arrived in England in April of 1998, shortly after Easter. Although my husband had "seen enough cathedrals to last a lifetime," on previous visits to Europe, he cheerfully indulged my first-timer's urge to check out every one along our route.

By the time we'd made two or three stops, I was entranced by a tradition I've never seen in the United States. Near the entrance of every church and cathedral stood an empty tomb. Some exhibits were large enough for a small child to enter, surrounded by potted plants and Easter lilies. Others were modest displays. They all contained the same elements—a rocky tomb, a rolled-away stone, a discarded white grave cloth and flowers.

My heart began following the empty tombs from city to city.

In the charming village of Bradford-Upon-Avon a British couple offered us a guided tour of their town. From our starting point at their centuries-old church we crossed the lane to a lumpish, ancient stone building—one of the oldest Norman churches in Britain. We made a brief, admiring circuit of the empty interior and stepped back into the entryway, toward the sunlight. Only then did I notice what I'd missed on the way in.

There, nestled in the corner of a stone bench in the entry alcove was a tiny empty tomb. I could almost have cradled it in the palms of my hands. Small pieces of slate formed the walls and roof. A flat stone stood off to one side. A snippet of white for a burial cloth. A sprig of ivy. Diminutive clumps of moss. Miniature clusters of flowers.

A story preserved for two millenia, retold without words, even in a church unused for centuries.

* * *

Today symbols rattle about in my head like marbles on an uneven floor. Some await a catalyst, a character or a story, to imbue them with meaning. Other symbols lodge in certain regions of my heart like showcased treasures, vibrant with significance of their own—symbols like a rainbow, a stable, a cross, an empty tomb.

Truth Lesson

It is a greater thing for me to comprehend a spiritual truth in my heart than for me to understand any number of related facts with my mind. It is through such non-rational wisdom that I most often grow in faith and in understanding of God's ever-present love.

Higher Spires

═══════════════════

A man complains to his wife as they leave a neat,
white traditional American church:
"If we don't start getting better results,
I'm thinking of trying one with a higher steeple."
Joe Martin
Mr. Boffo comic strip

Wesley's Chapel didn't stand a chance—not coming on
the heels of half a dozen cathedrals.

By the end of our second week in Great Britain, Pete and
I had walked miles beneath the soaring arches, stained glass
and echoing stones of cathedrals at Canterbury, Salisbury,
Wells. Our vacation was gaining momentum as we left
southern England and took a broad arc to the northwest.
From there we would return to London for our flight back to
the United States. I suppose we were feeling an unspoken
urgency toward home.

Bristol was among our final stops.

The guidebook I carried that afternoon grew limp in my

clenched hand as we ventured into a busy downtown thoroughfare. Open only to foot traffic, the broad street was lined by glitzy shops touting modern fashions. We threaded our way among rainbow crew cuts and punk rocker costumes. Frenetic pop music pumped from unseen speakers.

Nothing very spiritual here.

Doubtful, I checked the guidebook again. We asked directions of a young woman in a dress shop. She hadn't heard of the place.

About to give up, we decided to walk just a little further.

And there, in the midst of brash modern Bristol, stood the oldest Methodist building in the world, John Wesley's Chapel.

We passed through the gate at the street into a courtyard, leaving the 1990s cacophony behind. In the sudden quiet we passed a life-size equestrian statue of John Wesley astride his horse, Bible in hand—the original circuit rider, spreading the word of God.

I should have been prepared for the contrast as we approached the unassuming building at the end of the courtyard. I hardly expected a Protestant chapel of the 1700s to rival the spectacle of a medieval cathedral, but I was shocked by the stark simplicity as we opened the door and stepped inside.

The white rails of balconies extended like outstretched arms from the pulpit that loomed high above a small sea of dark wooden pews. No speck of color. No shard of stained glass. No carved stones underfoot. No towering arches above. No side chapels dedicated to saints or kings.

Wesley's Chapel was silent, neat, austere and empty except for Pete and me. *Bleak*, whispered a little voice in my ear, reminding me of the severities of early American Protestants in New England.

Could I backpedal toward the door quickly enough to leave before anyone knew I was there?

* * *

Churches have taken a bum rap for years.

People like me who operate on fuzzy logic tend to slather church structures with all sorts of negative baggage about organized religion. For years I equated the buildings with the shortcomings of the people who worshipped there. And I avoided churches for everything they seemed to represent.

My mother always contended that one didn't have to attend church to prove one's belief in God. I had plenty of other relatives and friends who felt the same. I was comfortable with that stance myself for much of my life.

As a teenager I found spirituality in nature. That's easy to do in the Pacific Northwest where snow-capped mountains embellish the horizons, crystal rivers churn toward the Pacific and breathtaking greenery proclaims the existence of a supreme being.

During my high school years I often visited Deception Pass, a dramatic spot thirty minutes from my home in Mt. Vernon, where the mainland fragments into the San Juan Islands. In the middle of the pass stands a small island with enough parking for a few cars and enough scenery for all comers. Sitting on that island hillside, riddled with adolescent angst, I watched the water rush and boil in furious currents below the bridge and poured out my heart in tortured poetry.

I believed then that I was drawn to Deception Pass to find myself.

I believe now that this wild and turbulent place was my first church.

* * *

Inside Wesley's Chapel Pete and I cleared our throats, fidgeted, glanced at each other. We saw no one else. We heard no voices. We could still make an escape without embarrassing ourselves.

But as much as I wanted to leave, I couldn't bring myself to do so. The Anglican cathedrals were magnificent, but John Wesley was the founder of my own faith tradition and this was a chance to explore my Methodist roots. Besides, on a purely practical note, we'd walked a good distance to find the Chapel. It seemed shallow and cowardly to give up over a dreary first impression.

The wooden floor creaked beneath my feet as I ventured forward and opened the low wooden door to one of the pews. Sitting down, I gazed up at the pulpit. I imagined Wesley, bewigged, berobed, exhorting me toward faithful living. I wondered if my back could withstand the pew's unforgiving right-angle construction for a whole sermon.

In hushed voices Pete and I agreed to climb the stairs to the living quarters. A sign told us we'd find a shop and museum there.

Upstairs we roamed through the history-laden rooms and marveled at the small size of the clerical robes preserved in a glass case. (Shouldn't giants of the faith be giants in stature as well?) We chatted with two congenial museum staffers and chose brochures and postcards to share with our Methodist friends at home.

To all appearances we were done, ready to retrace our steps through Bristol to our car.

Sensing some unfinished business I wandered back into John Wesley's quarters. Dutifully I noted the bed and the washstand, the labeled artifacts and pictures. Then I spotted a small side room I hadn't noticed before. This little room contained a stand-up desk by the window. A placard said that Wesley had worked here, penning his sermons and his journal entries.

I placed my hands upon the worn desktop and looked out the window. The view was unremarkable—just the rear of some other old buildings. Did Wesley see some of these same buildings as he worked? What was it like to be a religious revolutionary thinking and writing in this unadorned room? I ran my fingers over the surface of the desk. Then I saw the inviting indentation in the wooden footrest below.

I hesitated for just an instant.

My foot fit into place there just as easily as my feet had slipped into the hollowed stone steps of a cathedral a few days earlier.

For a moment I stood with John Wesley.

Monks and Methodists aren't that much different after all. Our feet are all pretty much the same size. Our feet are all pretty much pointed in the same direction.

* * *

Instructions for building a church: Entwine fingers, pointing downward, to form a flat-roofed building. Add a spire by pointing two index fingers upward in an inverted V. Hold upturned thumbs side by side to form a closed double door. At the appropriate time, spread open thumbs, upend hands and wiggle fingers.

> Here is the church.
> Here is the steeple.
> Open the doors
> and see all the people.

I hear happy laughter. Whose is it? Mine when my mother and father said the rhyme for me? Or is it my children chortling when I recited the rhyme for them?

For many years I didn't believe that church could be a place of laughter or joy. But church signs have helped change that misperception. A few months ago I arrived at the Lutheran church where I attend one of my regular Twelve Step meetings and chuckled at the message displayed on its sign for that week.

"You asked for a sign," it announced to passing motorists. "Well, here it is!"

* * *

In recent years I've come to love houses of worship. Maybe something in my heart compels me to make up for lost time.

During a single month last year I took midday communion with a dozen other men and women at the high altar in the National Cathedral in Washington D.C., attended a lively ecumenical service at an aging Catholic retreat center in Houston, worshipped with my father in his small town Assembly of God church in Washington, and attended Bay Harbour United Methodist Church in League City, Texas, where Pete and I are members.

I like the experience of being in churches. I like the solitude and quiet of my own church when everyone else is off about their weekday activities. I like visiting unfamiliar churches to see the familiar elements of faith—the altar, the pulpit, the cross—in endless expressions of material and design. Mostly I like what I've learned about church over the last few years.

Good churches never attempt to wall God in, claiming exclusivity.

Good churches never attempt to wall anyone out.

Good churches are as easily entered, as fluid and welcoming, as those childlike constructions of knuckles and palms.

* * *

Today I gravitate to churches because of the good intentions and the common convictions embraced there.

On our last wedding anniversary, which fell on a Sunday, Pete took me to dinner at a local hotel restaurant. As we entered the lobby we heard praise music coming from a non-denominational worship service underway in one of the hotel's conference rooms. We followed the music and paused to listen near the door. The ushers smiled and beckoned to us: "Come in. Come on in."

We smiled, shook our heads. No thanks. The moment didn't allow us to tell them we'd already spent a fine morning in church.

I would have liked to tell them that we were already walking a similar path.

In church I've discovered a dimension of faith that I once denied myself. As a young woman I believed that enough dedication to poetry and fiction could untangle my spiritual confusion and clarify the meaning for my life. I was as deluded as the sailors who once sailed into Deception Pass thinking it offered passage to somewhere other than Puget Sound. Instead of enlightenment, I found myself trapped in a lonely box of spiritual isolation.

Deception Pass was a beginning.

Years later the Twelve Steps opened the door.

Along with other Twelve Steppers I've often said that all it takes to start a new meeting is two people and a coffeepot. Today I hear in that statement the echo of words spoken more than two millenia ago: "When two or more are gathered in my name ..."

The parallel is significant.

I can't recover in isolation.

And I can't do church alone.

Church Lesson

There is much about houses of worship to inspire and advance my spiritual development. Church embraces any space that's dedicated to God, where people gather for a spiritual quest. In church the prayers of hundreds or thousands who've gone before me create a flowing stream of faith that bears me forward in my own journey.

Mystic Mentors

=====================================

"To rediscover the story of the Christian mystics is a great adventure. Their manifold experiences and examples can be truly empowering for our own lives."
Ursula King
Christian Mystics:
The Spiritual Heart of the Christian Tradition

Round and round the mulberry bush, the monkey chased the weasel. The monkey thought 'twas all in fun ...
An ice-cream truck yodeled its jarring melody above the rumble of Houston traffic, across the convent grounds, piercing the quiet of the room where I sat with two dozen other people, deep in centering prayer.
... POP goes the weasel!
Poof went my concentration. And up shot a flare of irritation.
I cherished the silence of my occasional twenty-four-hour prayer retreats at the convent. This was *my* time. How dare

such a commonplace racket intrude, even here?

Small rustlings around me. A few cleared throats.

I remained still, eyes closed, confident that we'd all remain faithful to our twenty-minute prayer commitment. But I couldn't regain focus. My mind refused to slip below the irksome tune.

Duh-da-duh, da-duh-dee-dee-duh. POP goes the weasel. Over and over and over.

Oh, great! Now my brain was humming along. I tried to shift in my chair without making any noise. I struggled to release the distraction.

Then a soft whisper in my mind yanked me out of my self-centered snit. *Are you forgetting how much I love children?*

Well, that was the last straw! Now I was talking to myself.

The whisper again: *Who says that prayer time must be shrouded in silence to be holy?*

Uh-oh. Was my pursuit of God turning me into a crotchety old lady? Was I slipping back into my old pattern of expectations and demands that life go my way?

I was still reflecting on those questions when the ice cream vendor switched off his warbling weasel song, revved up his engine and pulled away.

The quiet left behind pulsed with his absence.

* * *

"Have you read Thomas Merton's autobiography?" My friend John again.

While Merton's name sounded familiar, I hadn't read any of his work. John said he thought I'd find the book interesting because Merton had wandered far from religion before he eventually became a Trappist monk.

A short time later I found *The Seven Storey Mountain* in a used book store. I bought the book in spite of its forbidding aspect, and took it home, planning to give it a try.

That night in bed I read the opening sentence: "On the last day of January 1915, under the sign of the Water Bearer, in a year of a great war, and down in the shadow of some French mountain on the borders of Spain, I came into the world."

Oh, boy, I thought, *this is going to be a long haul.*

But I kept reading and by the time I laid aside the book to go to sleep, I was hooked.

Soon I was looking forward to bedtime because Merton's story waited by the bedside lamp. The deep texture of his writing impressed me. His honesty and insight exhilarated. Fascinated, I followed his long series of encounters with religion that laid the groundwork for his conversion to Catholicism and ultimately to his embracing monastic life.

I learned that during his youthful days of drinking, smoking and carousing with friends, Merton was an aspiring novelist. Yet even then he grappled with the meaning of the divine. "I remember how learnedly and enthusiastically I could talk for hours about mysticism and the experimental knowledge of God," he wrote, "and all the while I was stoking the fires of the argument with Scotch and soda."

* * *

One of my husbands (the first I think) claimed that I had no common sense. Typically he delivered this comment when my lack of comprehension about some business matter annoyed him.

I bristled at this unfair assessment of my intelligence. I didn't count it a serious shortcoming that I lacked the shrewdness he considered essential to survival in this world.

I do admit, however, that I'm attracted more to the spiritual than the tangible. This has prompted Gisela, my exceedingly practical friend, to remind me from time to time that it's fine to have my head in the clouds as long as I keep my feet on the ground.

I only wish that others could see how leaden and earthbound I feel. My feet are so deeply mired in this world that I must fight sometimes to achieve the smallest spiritual steps.

Perhaps that's why Merton's autobiography spoke to me in such a penetrating way.

After reading *The Seven Storey Mountain*, I sampled some of Merton's other work. Which led to books on contemplation and prayer by Thomas Keating and Basil Pennington. Which led to books about the saints and mystics. Which led to books *by* the saints and mystics. Which led to the convent where I joined others in contemplation, in centering prayer.

* * *

The example of the mystics has been enlightening for me. Their message is overwhelmingly one of love in action. Men and women who were transported by profound visions and deep mystical unions also led lives of dedicated service and sacrifice for others. In them I see that that love *of* God and love *from* God must play out as love for others here on earth, or it is barren.

In the mystics there is always the admonition to *do*. "The important thing is not to think much but to love much," wrote St. Teresa of Avila. I'm repeatedly reminded that my relationship with God may seem like a solitary activity, but prayer isn't meant to be an end in itself. The purpose of my relationship with God is to equip me to be a channel of his love into the world.

This means giving up all my *if onlys*.

If only I felt better physically ... Therese of Lisieux suffered cheerfully and almost silently as she died of tuberculosis at age 24.

If only I didn't have so many interruptions ... St. Catherine of Genoa found time between prayers to operate a hospital. St. Joan, between visions, fought to unify her nation and her people. Julian of Norwich, closeted as an anchorite in a tiny cell attached to a church, served as spiritual advisor to those who visited her there.

If only I could get away somewhere ... Thomas Merton "got away" to the silence of a monastery only to face his true calling, to spend his life pouring forth words, filling countless volumes, inspiring others onward in faith.

I'm finally receiving the message.

God wants me right where I am, when I am, who I am.

I need nothing I don't already have to live an increasingly spiritual life. A lengthy retreat would be nice. (I dream of a month on the Oregon coast.) Absolute silence would be, well, extraordinary. But if I hold out, waiting until the planets are in alignment or all the conditions of my life and environment reach perfection, I will never *get it*—whatever "it" turns out to be for me.

"Quiet days with God may be a snare," cautions Oswald Chambers. "We have to pitch our tents where we shall always have quiet times with God, however noisy our times with the world may be."

I suppose I expected the mystics to teach me about silence and seclusion. The introvert within me hoped for that. But even the reclusive desert fathers and mothers of the early centuries were sought out by others for their teachings. For the most part I've discovered that the mystics underwent great hardships to meld the love of God with the practical needs of the world.

They tell me I can't expect transport into some protected realm. They tell me that God prizes my honest efforts to connect with him in the clamor of daily life—in the press at a security checkpoint in a crowded airport, in the honking, creeping traffic of rush hour, in the joyful tumult of children converging on a callioped ice cream truck.

Pop goes the weasel.

Mystic Lesson

I once believed that I needed abundant leisure to get tight with God. As I study the lives of the saints and mystics I see wondrous examples of faith at work in the midst of life's most pressing demands. This offers infinite hope and encouragement for those like me who possess more earth-bound gifts.

Gargoyles On Duty

———

"Self searching is the means by which we bring new
vision, action, and grace to bear upon the dark and
negative side of our natures."
Twelve Steps and Twelve Traditions

A couple of years ago Pete and I were shopping for
Christmas gifts when he found me admiring a small, gray,
stuffed creature with horns, batwings, gigantic claws and
ominous teeth. I held it up for him to admire.

He backed away with a shudder.

My husband is so positive about life that I've found few
things about which he's less than enthusiastic. I made a
mental note to add gargoyles to the short list and returned
the winsome critter to the shelf, abandoning my notion of
taking it home to perch on my desk.

A week or two later as I browsed in a mall for some last
minute gifts, I happened upon a colorful display of books for
children. A slender picture book caught my eye with a vivid,
stained-glass cover illustration and ironic title: *God Bless*

the Gargoyles.

I skimmed the story on the spot.

Grinning, I tucked the book under my arm and headed for the checkout line.

* * *

If you had asked me at any time before I found the Twelve Step programs, I would have said without hesitation that I was a positive person. I honestly believed that was true. But as I worked the Twelve Steps and listened to hundreds of people talk about their lives, I realized that I'd been controlled by negativity for years—including a spectrum of fears and their common manifestation, worry.

My mother had elevated worry to an art form. I followed suit. Even before I was grown, I thought there was something wrong with lighthearted people. Couldn't they take things seriously? Didn't they understand how grave this business of living could be? Didn't they know that if you weren't careful you might trip and fall, miss the bus, get your dress dirty, poke your eye out?

As far as I was concerned happy-go-lucky meant irresponsible. It never occurred to me that I might learn some pointers by observing positive people and their approaches to life.

Learning to internalize my emotions, I lived with stress and an ongoing string of illnesses. As a young mother I obsessed about terrible things that might befall my husband or children. In bed at night I could magnify an imaginary scenario to awesome proportions, assuring myself of little sleep.

By the time I reached the Twelve Steps it was clear that living on the worried side of life wasn't working very well.

In recovery I heard this admonition: *Your mind is like a dangerous neighborhood. Don't go there alone!* For a negative thinker like me this was valuable and practical advice.

The implied meaning was that I should test ideas and plans with a sponsor or other advisor. But most important, I could and should take God into my thoughts.

In a wonderful little book, *Christ-Following: Ten Signposts to Spirituality*, Trevor Hudson writes that people of faith often acknowledge only the acceptable parts of their personalities. We neglect or reject our "shadow selves," he says. But when we deny those aspects of ourselves, "large tracts of our inner life are prevented from experiencing God's transforming friendship. Conversion can only continue as we acknowledge these shadow selves and expose them to the light of God's love."

Happily the Twelve Steps offered my shadow selves nowhere to hide. The inventory process revealed all my counter-productive thought patterns and the pessimistic corners of my character. Wide open for examination, I learned that I had some choices about what went on in my brain.

I could refuse to indulge in resentful imaginings about other people. I could avoid sensational news stories that contributed to frightening fantasies. I could separate phantom worries from real concerns, discarding the first and taking appropriate action on the second.

And I could put God thoughts in place of free-floating anxieties. I *could* reorient myself toward optimism.

A few years into recovery I realized that I was seldom ill anymore.

* * *

My sponsor Carol A. once gave me an assignment. "Watch Sandi," she said. "Listen to what she says and how she handles life. I don't expect you to become like her. But Sandi doesn't view everything with the deadly seriousness that you do. It might help you see things in a more positive light."

Everyone loved Sandi, including me, so the assignment

was a pleasant one. Relentlessly cheerful at meetings, Sandi always wore a smile. Even when she was embroiled in career or relationship problems, her upbeat style and sense of humor made everyone laugh. Watching her I learned to laugh at myself and to recognize the mountainous molehills I sometimes produced in my own path.

I was still learning from Sandi when she contracted ovarian cancer. Over the next three years her spirited newsletters kept friends up to date on her treatments and her condition until she was finally too weak to continue.

Sandi died several years ago. Carol A. died a year later. But even now if my dark side threatens to drag me down into negativity, worry, self-pity or any other futile state of mind, I remember Carol's advice. I can still watch Sandi, if only in my mind.

Today I have a new role model. Snakes and gargoyles aside, one of my husband's most admirable qualities is incontrovertible optimism.

* * *

On Christmas morning, we opened all our real, grown-up presents and then I handed Pete a thin, square package.

"Hmmm." He hefted it, felt the edges. "Must be a book." Stripping away the paper, he looked at the title and laughed.

Like all good fiction *God Bless the Gargoyles* contains some truth. Author Dav Pilkey tells how gargoyles were perched high on cathedrals to keep away evil spirits, but over the centuries people came to fear them, hating their ugly presence on the house of God. In Pilkey's story the misunderstood gargoyles weep with sorrow until angels come to comfort them and take them on a winged night tour.

So if you see shapes in the night sky, don't fear —
for it simply means angels and gargoyles are near,

easing the earth with their gentle night call:
"God bless the gargoyles. God bless us all."

Finally I have a gargoyle of my own. A gift from Pete.
As I write, my gray stone friend leans over me intently, elbows propped on my computer, jowls resting in clawed hands, wings swept back over haunches. My extra pair of glasses give him an owlish, intelligent look. We gaze at each other whenever I'm stuck on a phrase or trying to untangle a snarled passage in my work.

My gargoyle is heavy, substantial, dependable, ready to ward off any demons that might find their way into my office. And he keeps me in touch with myself. His fearsome exterior gives a face to my internal gloom, reflecting the part of me that's frightening when kept in shadow, the part that wants to hide from God as unworthy, the part that most needs to be presented to God for transformation.

Besides all that, he makes me smile.

Among the gargoyles atop the National Cathedral in Washington D.C. is a stone replica of Darth Vader, embodiment of human darkness and nemesis of Luke Skywalker in the movie series *Star Wars*. A modern gargoyle like Darth Vader reminds me that human nature is the same yesterday, today and tomorrow.

The gargoyle on my computer reminds me that God knows everything there is to know about me ... and loves me still.

Negativity Lesson

The dark aspect of my character is an inescapable part of human nature. It may lie dormant for long periods but, in times of spiritual weakness or confusion, may awaken again. Yet the darkness can never control me if I claim it, draw it out and present it for the healing touch of God.

Boppin' Theophanies

"We can all see God in exceptional things, but it requires
the culture of spiritual discipline to see God in every detail.
Never allow that the haphazard is anything less than
God's appointed order, and be ready to discover
the Divine designs anywhere."
Oswald Chambers
My Utmost for His Highest

It didn't surprise us that we couldn't spot the comet.

Neither Pete nor I had high expectations of seeing much
besides overcast when we parked our rental car on the crest
of a hill and stepped out to search the evening sky. It was
worth checking, but we agreed after a few minutes that it
was pointless to linger.

Soon we were back in our car, heading down the hill
toward Interstate 5, leaving Mt. Vernon, Washington, where
we'd been visiting my family. Our flight back to Houston
was scheduled to leave Seattle early the next morning.

Beginning the hour's drive, we talked about family and

friends and projects that awaited us at home. From time to time, I glanced out the car window at the sky. I hadn't quite let go of my disappointment that we'd missed the much-heralded spectacle of a comet. (We'd failed to see the comet from Houston as well.) And now we were even going to miss a total lunar eclipse—due to begin soon, somewhere out there beyond the clouds.

* * *

The Twelve Step programs are a great place to learn about miracles. If I attend a meeting in a grumpy mood I'm almost certain to hear a God-at-work story that rekindles my sense of gratitude.

The typical Twelve Step miracle is seldom drawn from a spiritual mountaintop. Most emerge from daily life. And the recognition of a Higher Power at work often starts with the small stuff—"It was pouring rain and a parking place opened up for me right in front of the door!" or "God helped me find my keys and showed me a way around that traffic jam so I got to the job interview right on time!"

But typically, as recovery progresses, stories move beyond these training wheel miracles to more profound awareness of a benevolent spiritual presence in the world. I've heard wonderful stories ... from a man who wiped away tears as he told of surprising his small grandchildren with gifts from his woodworking shop, from a woman who spoke of reconciling with her estranged mother before her mother died, from a man who described with awe his first visit to the ocean.

My personal definition of a miracle, shaped through my Twelve Step recovery: any experience or awareness that helps one grow closer to God.

One of my earliest miracles was a garden.

* * *

I was new to recovery, working my way through the Twelve Steps for the first time, when I decided to plant a flower garden. As an adult I'd always lived in rented houses or apartments but my second husband and I had recently bought a home in Dallas where the lush back yard bore witness to the previous owner's green thumb. As winter drew to an end, a plot of bare ground between the berry bushes and the pear tree began to beckon me.

I knew that ten by twelve patch had been a vegetable garden most recently. While I'm a big fan of veggies, the produce aisle in the grocery store has ample variety for me.

But flowers! Now *there* was an exhilarating thought.

I'd grown up surrounded by the glorious blooms of my mother's and grandmothers' gardens. I'd sipped the nectar from Mother's nasturtiums, held heart-to-heart conversations with Grandma's snapdragons and, when I was five, hung out with the giant sunflowers in our yard until I was stung by a couple of disgruntled bees.

Flowers it would be.

It never occurred to me that I might fail as a gardener—even though the only plants that had ever thrived in my care were cacti and succulents that flourished mostly from benign neglect.

I could do this.

At that time, my life in recovery still seemed so foreign—with its routine of meetings, daily study of the Twelve Steps, phone calls to a sponsor—that planning a garden was just one more strange new activity to add to my days. I pored over seed catalogues, debated the merits of annuals and perennials and sketched planting diagrams that would suit the flowers I liked best.

I planted my garden on Easter weekend. Coincidence? Probably not. Although it was several years before I would venture near a church, the hope embodied in Easter and spring seemed particularly timely as I entrusted my carefully selected seeds to my new God and to the ground.

Then I watered and weeded and waited.

I was thrilled when tiny shoots of green emerged, spellbound as the plants shot up into the air. It was a garden to beat all gardens. I never tired of admiring it, walking the rows, pulling stray weeds and watching the marvel as promising buds burst into bloom.

I have a photograph of me in the midst of my garden with marigolds clustered at my feet, zinnias and cosmos brushing my legs, the dinner-plate blossoms of sunflowers towering over me.

For family and friends, my gardening adventure must have been entertaining to watch. One relative laughed about my sunflowers. "They grow wild all over the place in Texas," she teased. "People mow them down here, Connie. They're weeds!"

Ah, but I'd seen those rangy little roadside sunflowers. Mine were different. Mine were the giants that my mother had grown. Mine were part of my recovery.

For an experienced gardener familiar with seeds and soil and sunshine, I suppose that summer of 1982 was a year like dozens of others. But for me, testing the resilience of my brand new faith, every hour spent turning the soil, planting the seeds, tending and rejoicing, was an earthly revelation of an entirely new, totally unexplored spiritual realm.

For me, my garden was a miracle.

* * *

It was dark that evening when Pete and I reached the northern outskirts of Seattle. Millions of lights blanketed the landscape in a high-energy display that tugged my attention away from the sky. I gave up any lingering hope of seeing astronomical wonders. Everyone knows that stargazing is best done away from cities.

I began thinking about our flight the next morning and the half-finished articles that awaited me on my desk at home. Then, glancing out the window at the twinkling cityscape, I suddenly realized the sky over Seattle (wonder of wonders) wasn't overcast at all.

It was clear and luminous with stars. Clear! Stars!

Well, what about *comets*? What about *eclipses*?

Quickly I scanned the sky.

There, far off in the west, high above the city lights, much too chubby to be a star, trailing its telltale tail, the Hale-Bopp Comet chugged southward in the western sky. I swung around in my seat to peer out Pete's window. There in the east, a plump silver moon, suspended just above the buildings of Bellevue, slowly succumbed to darkness as the Earth's creeping shadow blocked off the sunlight.

Pete, look! Out your window. Out mine. I can't believe it!

Eventually my babbling trailed off into silence. This was too magnificent for a barrage of feeble words.

We flowed on through the city, moving with traffic, suspended in time. On our left the Earth overshadowed the moon as it's done for eons. On our right a visitor comet hurtled through blackness, just passing by on its way to places of which I could only dream.

Arriving at the motel near Sea-Tac Airport, I reluctantly retrieved my suitcase from the trunk of the car and followed Pete inside. It was hard to leave the moment behind. We'd just spent half an hour bracketed by celestial grandeur. And I would never—at least not in this lifetime—see anything like that again.

* * *

A few months before the turn of the century, after years of

emotional foot-dragging and vocal resistance, I finally upgraded my geriatric 1986 office technology to bigger, better, brighter, light-years-faster equipment. Once I moved past my grudging acceptance of the new computer, I gave us both a present—a nifty screensaver with photos taken by the Hubble telescope.

For the wallpaper behind the Windows icons on my screen I chose a resplendent shot of the Cygnus Loop, the colorful remnant of an ancient supernova. Now when I turn on my computer, I can admire the abstract patterns of the gaseous debris flung into space by an ancient cataclysm. For a moment I might even consider larger questions than whether or not an editor has responded to my e-mail.

Astronomy has always challenged my liberal arts mentality. For the most part I'm content with a gee-whiz-lookit-that approach to the universe, leaving it to the astrophysicists and cosmologists to sort out the latest theories of creation.

I follow astronomy because it inspires me Godward.

I love the headlines—*Another Solar System Discovered, New Data Detects Existence of Black Holes, Telescopes Probe the Boundary of Universe.* Astronomers have even detected a tantalizing hiss, a sound they say may date from the absolute beginning.

I don't need a radio telescope or recording equipment to confirm such a discovery for myself—simply the certainty in my heart that allows me to recognize the whisper of creation, the poetry of the divine.

* * *

Occasionally I'm guilty of spiritual envy—imagining the grass to be greener somewhere else.

Is it easier for astronauts to be persons of faith?

Is it simpler for cloistered monks and nuns to feel the presence of God?

Is the Hale-Bopp Comet even now streaking toward a space that is closer to God than where I am? When such questions intrude, I remind myself that *where* I am, *when* I am and *who* I am is probably just what should be going on at this point in my life. I believe that as I move forward in my unique personal journey, God is just as present to me as my developing comprehension allows him to be.

God was as near as the profusion of flowers in my Dallas garden. He's as near as every miracle story I hear in Twelve Step meetings. He's as near as my desktop when my computer crackles to life and splashes a supernova across my screen.

And every now and then God delivers a big one.

Mine came one dazzling night in Seattle, on March 23, 1997, when God passed a shadowy hand over the moon and sent a comet be-Bopp'n across the heavens, a stunning reminder that he's unrestrained by any confines imposed by the human mind.

Miracle Lesson

God lavishes me with miracles large and small. My response to theophanies should be increased humility and renewed devotion to this generous creator who continues to astonish me with progressive and persistent revelations of his magnificence and his love.

Christian Under Construction

"Give our Lord the benefit of believing
that his hand is leading you and accept
the anxiety of feeling yourself in
suspense and incomplete."
Teilhard de Chardin

I was apprehensive when I arrived at the convent on
Friday evening and opened the massive wooden door to
carry my overnight bag inside. After this weekend the nuns
were closing the retreat center for renovations. An eight-
month hiatus between prayer retreats seemed to me like a
long, long time.

Checking in with the receptionist in the lofty ceilinged
foyer, I said yes, I've been there before so I knew the drill. I
repeated my assigned room number and followed a hallway
toward the stairs.

On the third floor I located the room where a computer-generated card with my name hung from a clip on the door-frame below a picture of St. Teresa of Avila. Ah, Teresa again. On my last visit I'd stayed in another room that bore her name. Teresa had been one of my mentors in recent months and it was reassuring to know that a divine instinct was guiding the hand that made room assignments.

I smiled, remembering my first visit. That day Sister Mary Tobin had escorted me to a corner room which I'd like to believe is reserved for first-time visitors. The name on that door: Mary the Mother of God.

The nuns have been taking good care of me.

I placed my overnight bag inside the small, spotless room and closed the door. As I drew the window blinds I looked down through the gathering dusk at my car parked in the circular drive below. It seemed to belong to a different world.

My room contained a narrow bed, a simple nightstand and lamp, a small armchair, a built-in desk with shelves above, a straight chair. A rack on the wall held a pink bath towel with matching hand towel and washcloth.

The closet's single sliding door moved in one direction to reveal a clothes rod with hangers, the other direction to reveal a built-in chest of drawers with a drinking glass, coffee mug and mirror on top. I opened the drawers to locate the extra blanket and fresh linens I would use to remake my bed and restock the towel rack the next day before departing. The linens were deliciously soft, the sheets pastel with a tiny flowered design, the towels, sturdy and well-washed, all smooth and comforting to the touch.

I placed my clothes in the closet, my nightgown on the bed, my alarm clock on the bedside table. I removed from the pillow the gentle reminders about the silent nature of the retreat and the housekeeping routine for guests.

Like all retreatant rooms here, mine had lights everywhere. A fixture provided light in the closet. A switch at the door operated a florescent light above the bed. A lamp stood on the bedside table. Another florescent tube furnished light for the desk.

Clearly, this was a room for reading, study and illumination.

On the shelf above the desk a picture of Teresa of Avila stood in solitary simplicity. *"God withholds himself from no one who perseveres."* I placed my Bible, my Twelve Step books, my notebook and pen on the desk and switched on the light.

Then I turned to the crucifix that hung on the wall between the windows.

The bare linoleum of the floor felt wonderfully cool to my knees and to the tops of my pampered Protestant feet.

* * *

A former pastor at my church once preached a sermon that began like this: A woman was shopping for a cross in a jewelry store when the eager salesclerk displayed a variety of designs for her to consider. "Oh, no," the woman exclaimed, pushing away a modern cross formed of intersecting nails. "I don't like that one at all. I don't want any nails in my cross."

The rest of that sermon is forgotten, but not its incisive message.

Imagine Christianity without nails.

Before I became "religious," even before I became "spiritual," I was reasonably comfortable with the Protestant cross. Simple, uncluttered, uncomplicated, it felt familiar from my Sunday School days.

The crucifix, on the other hand, was more than a little disconcerting. It seemed a morbid instrument for pummeling the viewer with guilt. Who needed a barbaric reminder of unspeakable sacrifice? Who wanted to see agony, dying, death?

In 1997 I attended a life-changing spiritual retreat. The event took place in a cramped and creaky facility with unpredictable plumbing, wobbly bunk beds and an outdated kitchen that served up bounteous meals to fuel a three-day emotional roller coaster. Late one night, exhausted by another spiritual upheaval, I sat in a pew in the little Catholic chapel and gazed at the crucifix high above the altar.

Suddenly I understood.

In the form of Jesus on the cross I glimpsed the sheer depth of love that lies at the heart of Christianity. I realized that to understand the power of the resurrection, I must first embrace the reality and significance of Christ's death. And at that moment I knew that Christianity not only entails my acceptance of God's love, but my emulating Christ's selflessness in thanks for what I've been given.

Christianity has *never* been about comfort.

Christianity has *always* been about nails.

* * *

Many years ago my mother moved from her home near Seattle to Alaska. During her first winter in Anchorage she was puzzled by a major construction project downtown shrouded in enormous sheets of plastic. When spring came she wrote about the strange spectacle as workers released the protective sheathing to reveal a finished building.

Cocoons come in many shapes and forms.

In Twelve Step recovery people often joke about the embarrassment of growing up in public—the belated maturing that takes place through working the steps. How much more comfortable it would be to hide away one's unfinished self and emerge in due time, transformation complete.

As I fretted about the renovations at the convent, I began to question the motives underlying my concern. Why did I return to the convent like a homing pigeon whenever my schedule permitted? (I was clearly too old, too married, too Protestant to become a nun.) Was I cocooning in its sanctuary? Was I swaddling myself in spiritual cotton as I passed through a new phase of growth?

My misgivings about the renovations seemed shamelessly self-serving. I didn't want anything at the retreat center to change. I loved the prayer room, the icon room, the listening room where retreatants donned headphones to hear audiotapes. I loved the simplicity of the guest rooms and the echoey bathrooms with their multitude of private nooks and crannies. I loved the spaces and the silence.

Was I afraid I'd find no silence or serenity elsewhere during the months the retreat center was closed?

During a conference with Sister Adeline, I asked about the remodeling. She said the work would be centered in the nuns' residential quarters, plus a much-needed redo of the air conditioning system which would render the entire third floor uninhabitable during the heat of a Houston summer and fall.

Good news! This wasn't about change after all. This was about climate control.

Then I learned that many of the nuns would be uprooted, moving to other living quarters for the duration. Abashed, I promised to pray for the sisters during their absence.

In my room afterward I gazed at the small figure hanging wordlessly on the wall.

Give me a pull-no-punches crucifix to yank me back to solid ground whenever I'm about to be swamped by the riptide of self.

* * *

The first time I visited the National Cathedral in Washington D.C. in the mid-1970s, it was still under construction, a process that extended from the laying of the foundation stone in 1907 to its consecration in 1990.

Many of the English cathedrals I visited in 1997 were centuries in the building. Some rose up on earlier foundations. Some were expansions of primitive cores. Several cathedrals I saw were festooned with modern scaffolding as they underwent reinforcements and repairs.

What makes me think I must be completed overnight? I try to be patient, as well as persistent, about my faltering progress. I know the hardest part only *seems* to be the waiting. The real work of my spiritual growth actually lies far beyond my expertise or control.

Fortunately I know an excellent carpenter.

Construction Lesson

Spiritually I am a work in progress and will continue so until I die. At times, all I see is chaos because the master plan is obscured by the disorder of daily life. Still I must submit myself to this divine work on a daily basis without resisting the nails it takes to create a sturdy structure of my soul.

More God

"The voice of God hardly ever is found in complete paragraphs. The summons of God is heard in that place
called desire: the human heart."
Michael Downey
Trappist: Living in the Land of Desire

Once upon a time there was a foolish fish who lived in the
sprawling expanse of a great and wondrous ocean. She
swam about oblivious to her surroundings, giving other fish
the brush off when they tried to draw her attention to the
environment. Then one day, swimming for her life from a
bottom-dweller that threatened to devour her, she blundered
into a deep and rushing current. Twisting, turning, mar-
veling at the powerful embrace, she laughed in excitement.
"Look," she exclaimed to anyone who would listen,
"Wouldja look at this! I've discovered water!"

* * *

At the convent where I attend prayer retreats, a trail strikes off into the woods where one can wander for time alone. A series of rough-hewn crosses stand at intervals along the path. On examination, the crosses are simply sections of small tree limbs, cut to varied lengths and bolted together. The largest cross, about six feet tall, dominates the end of a cul-de-sac where the path loops off to one side.

New visitors might discount the cul-de-sac as an aimless detour.

One weekend last spring after passing the other crosses along the trail, I followed the loop in the path. As I stopped before the tall cross, a scurrying movement drew my attention to the sandy ground.

A horde of ants had constructed a path of their own across the trail. Their route was a tunnel with skylights every few inches—perhaps for air circulation or maybe because their roof had caved in. Through the holes, I could see a rushing, stumbling throng.

At first glance the track of the ants appeared bizarre. Originating somewhere in the weeds not far from the cross, it struck out away from the cross, traversing the walking path. Abruptly, just before reaching the far side of the trail, the tunnel made a sharp dogleg and turned back on itself, heading in the opposite direction.

Straight toward the cross.

I crouched in the path a distance away and watched the ants tramping along their perforated passage. The roof of the tunnel above the turn remained intact so I could only guess what altered their direction. Was an obstruction hidden in their path? Or was their change of direction in response to a new, intuitive call?

I looked up at the cross that stood above us, rugged and eloquent.

And I looked back down at the tiny ants. I wasn't surprised that they had expended so much time and energy rushing off in a meaningless direction. Hadn't I done the same? For me, their roundabout journey needed no explanation.

The cross was simply too enormous for them to see.

* * *

So what has become of the woman who once bristled at the mention of God and was embarrassed to pray? Who is this woman who hops out of bed eagerly at six on Sunday mornings in order to spend several hours in worship, study and fellowship with friends at church?

I'm grateful that God is loving, forgiving, endlessly patient and willing to be amused.

Now and then I wonder what my life would be like if I had come to faith earlier. But I am convinced that every part of my past, every halting step has been necessary to make me who I am today ...and who I am becoming. I doubt that my relationship with God would be nearly so precious if I hadn't tried to live without it first.

I remember the beating of my forlorn heart.

Today after twenty years in Twelve Step recovery and ten years in church, spirituality and religion have merged for me into one compelling quest for God.

In the process I've learned that this pilgrimage is not meant to be taken alone. I spend time in reading, writing, private prayer and meditation. But I also grow in community with others—sharing with other Twelve Steppers through meetings and sponsoring, learning from the ministers and studying with the congregation at my church, encouraging my family and friends in their faith journeys and allowing them to encourage, challenge and inspire me.

Spirituality shared is magnified.

* * *

In recent years I've been dreaming about houses. Sprawling hotel-like buildings. Bunker-like structures. Absurdly convoluted and complicated homes. Many are teeming with people and activities. A few (only a few) have attics or mysterious corridors with rooms I'm afraid to enter. My dream dictionary tells me my subconscious is examining my life.

My latest dream involved a living room devoid of furniture and details except for high windows along three sides and a series of dark objects that hung from the ceiling. Throughout my dream, although I returned repeatedly to that room, everything remained unchanged until just before I awoke. Then the high windows stood open and a breeze whipped through the room stirring all the objects at the ceiling.

Wind chimes! Rows and rows of wind chimes!

I stood in the center of the room, turning, looking, listening as the room reverberated with music.

Today I am no longer the little girl wondering what to do with the *talent* I was given in Sunday School or the young woman who resisted faith because I didn't know where or how to begin. I am a woman richly gifted by an inspired recovery program and inflamed by the guidance of those ahead of me toward a greater, deeper, fuller experience of God.

Today I long to know more God, to share more God.

Now the windows of my heart are open, now the spirit blows freely through my life, my soul is singing.

Semi-Final Lesson

God is and was, long before I settled on that truth. My former life convinced me that the way of self leads to cosmic loneliness. Today I know that the way of God strengthens my heart, nourishes my spirit and refines my soul for each day's challenges, for my life's work and, I trust, for whatever may lie ahead.

Afterword

I have an abiding concern for readers who may find themselves turning the final page of my book, wanting more God for themselves and wondering how to proceed. When I attended my first Twelve Step meeting in 1981, I had no inkling that 20 years later I would be a Christian Twelve Stepper, or any sense of how slow, sometimes frustrating, sometimes joyful, my journey would be. And while my transformation continues today, it's clearly my own unique evolution, not meant to be duplicated by others.

That said, I'll offer a few parting suggestions for the reader who senses Christianity beckoning.

What I have to say will sound suspiciously similar to the five admonitions that hang on the walls of many Twelve Step recovery meeting rooms. (Don't practice your addiction. Go to meetings. Read the *Big Book*. Associate with recovering people. And pray.) The likeness is deliberate.

My suggestions: Don't practice judgmentalism toward religion or religious people. Go to church. Read the Bible and other spiritual literature. Associate with positive Christians. And pray.

Be prepared to visit a number of churches and attend a

variety of worship services. (If you're in recovery, chances are you didn't click right away with the first group or meeting you attended.) Keep in mind that it's probably not the worship service, but small group participation that will help you feel at home in church. A Bible study might be a good place to begin. Like the Big Book, the Bible may be read alone, but it's not meant to be interpreted in a vacuum.

And don't expect to meet saintly people in church. Sincere Christians grapple with personal shortcomings and the problems of living just like honest Twelve Steppers do. I speak from experience and observation in both settings.

Above all, ask God to clarify your spiritual path and direct your growth. While you may be surrounded, encouraged, even prodded by others, this is, after all, the most personal, and the most precious, of all journeys.

As you pray for yourself, I will be praying for you too.

C.B.

The Twelve Steps of Alcoholics Anonymous

1. We admitted we were powerless over alcohol—that our lives had become unmanageable.
2. Came to believe that a Power greater than ourselves could restore us to sanity.
3. Made a decision to turn our will and our lives over to the care of God *as we understood Him*.
4. Made a searching and fearless moral inventory of ourselves.
5. Admitted to God, to ourselves, and to another human being the exact nature of our wrongs.
6. Were entirely ready to have God remove all these defects of character.
7. Humbly asked Him to remove our shortcomings.
8. Made a list of all persons we had harmed, and became willing to make amends to them all.
9. Made direct amends to such people wherever possible, except when to do so would injure them or others.
10. Continued to take personal inventory and when we were wrong promptly admitted it.
11. Sought through prayer and meditation to improve our conscious contact with God *as we understood Him*, praying only for knowledge of His will for us and the power to carry that out.
12. Having had a spiritual awakening as the result of these steps, we tried to carry this message to alcoholics, and to practice these principles in all our affairs.

The Twelve Steps are reprinted with permission of
Alcoholics Anonymous World Services, Inc. (A.A.W.S.)
Permission to reprint the Twelve Steps does not mean that
A.A.W.S. has reviewed or approved the contents of this publication, or that A.A.W.S. necessarily agrees with the views
expressed herein. A.A. is a program of recovery from alco-
holism *only*—use of the Twelve Steps in connection with
programs and activities which are patterned after A.A., but
which address other problems, or in any other non-A.A.
context, does not imply otherwise. Additionally, while A.A.
is a spiritual program, A.A. is not a religious program. Thus,
A.A. is not affiliated or allied with any sect, denomination,
or specific religious belief.

Printed in the United States
3509